ADVENTUROUS PUB WALKS
IN
NOTTINGHAMSHIRE

Peter Fooks

COUNTRYSIDE BOOKS

NEWBURY BERKSHIRE

COUNTRYSIDE BOOKS
3 Catherine Road
Newbury, Berkshire

To view our complete range of books,
please visit us at
www.countrysidebooks.co.uk

ISBN 1 85306 838 1

Designed by Peter Davies, Nautilus Design
Maps and photographs by the author
Cover photograph of the Vale of Belvoir
supplied by Derek Forss

Produced through MRM Associates Ltd., Reading
Typeset by Techniset Typesetters, Newton-le-Willows
Printed by Woolnough Bookbinding Ltd., Irthlingborough

CONTENTS

AREA MAP SHOWING THE LOCATION OF THE WALKS

INTRODUCTION

What exactly constitutes an 'adventurous walk'? A lot depends, I suppose, on your definition of 'adventure'. My own view, for what it is worth, is that any new and challenging experience can qualify – and I have enjoyed plenty of those in the preparation of this work.

There was a challenge of sorts in the project itself. Twenty walks of seven to twelve miles or so, to be surveyed in detail, problems ironed out, route and additional detail written up, legible sketch maps prepared, and everything checked and double-checked ready for submission to the publisher; all within the space of nine months or so.

Well, I never could resist a challenge. I have explored the Trent Valley, the Dukeries, Sherwood, the Vale of Belvoir and the South Nottinghamshire Wolds. I have walked in the footsteps of D. H. Lawrence, William Mompesson, Lifeguardsman John Shaw, William Brewster – and Robin Hood. And the whole experience has been one extended and joyous adventure.

None of these walks could be described as a gentle after dinner stroll, but neither should they pose any problems for persons of normal, average fitness. The length of a walk is not necessarily the sole criterion of difficulty, and most of these routes contain an element of challenge, even if it is nothing more than tracing a little-used path across an over-blown field of rape, or coping with a broken-down stile.

A reasonable, sustained walking pace, even where it includes uncomplicated paths and roads, will be about two miles an hour, to which must be added the time taken resting, picnicking, pausing for breath or 'admiring the scenery'. A 12-mile walk can be expected to take *at least* six hours, and then some. Say seven, to be safe. For this reason, most of the walks have been planned on the principle that a lunch break will be required part way around the route.

Because of this, it will clearly not be appropriate to park at the chosen pub. Where possible, I have recommended a public parking area, but it may be necessary, in some cases, to park by the roadside. Where this is the case, always ensure that you park tidily and considerately – and not where you shouldn't.

All of the pubs have been checked out and found satisfactory, both for the standard of service and the quality of the food and drink. There are considerable differences, however, in opening times, so be sure to check the details in the book before you start out.

Most of the walks, inevitably, follow vehicular roads for short stretches. Where this occurs, keep to the right-hand side of the road, and as close in to the edge as possible. Some of our Nottinghamshire roads are very busy, and blind bends are not uncommon. Always keep to the line of the path while crossing farmland, keep the dog under control, and leave gates as you find them. And if you decide to picnic, don't forget to take your litter home.

You will obviously dress according to the prevailing weather conditions: light clothing in summer and heavier stuff in winter. But be prepared for eventualities, with spare warm clothing in season, and waterproofs at all times. Several walkers these days wear shorts. I don't myself, simply because I am wary of overgrown footpaths, and I don't like stinging nettles! Proper walking boots or shoes are advisable too – and be prepared to remove them, if muddy, before entering the pub. A small first aid kit is worth packing in your rucksack, and plenty of liquid (non-alcoholic, of course!).

Have a good day now!

Peter Fooks

PUBLISHER'S NOTE

We hope that you obtain considerable enjoyment from this book; great care has been taken in its preparation. Although at the time of publication all routes followed public rights of way or permitted paths, diversion orders can be made and permissions withdrawn.

We cannot, of course, be held responsible for such diversion orders and any inaccuracies in the text which result from these or any other changes to the routes nor any damage which might result from walkers trespassing on private property. We are anxious though that all details covering the walks are kept up to date and would therefore welcome information from readers which would be relevant to future editions.

The simple sketch maps that accompany the walks in this book are based on notes made by the author whilst checking out the routes on the ground. They are designed to show you how to reach the start, to point out the main features of the overall circuit and they contain a progression of numbers that relate to the paragraphs of the text.

However, for the benefit of a proper map, we do recommend that you purchase the relevant Ordnance Survey sheet covering your walk. The Ordnance Survey maps are widely available, especially through booksellers and local newsagents.

WISE MEN'S WAYS AROUND GOTHAM

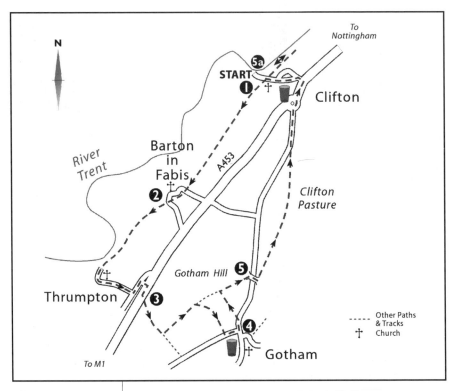

Distance:
10 (or 12) miles

Starting point:
River users' car
park, Holgate,
Clifton.
(Grid reference:
SK 541349)

Maps: OS Landranger 129 (Nottingham and Loughborough)
OS Explorer 260 (Nottingham and the Vale of Belvoir)

How to get there: *From Nottingham, follow the A453
south, turning right at Clifton Green and continuing
through the village. The car park is on the right, opposite
the hall and church.*

HOLGATE IN CLIFTON, ONE OF NOTTINGHAMSHIRE'S PRETTIEST VILLAGES

*C*lifton village, where this walk begins, has long been regarded as one of Nottinghamshire's prettiest. Despite some modern features, it retains much traditional beauty. After descending to the riverside, we follow the Trent Greenway, passing Holme Pit – a delightfully landscaped water feature – to arrive at Barton in Fabis. The riverside is rejoined at Thrumpton, from where we ascend the wooded Gotham Hill, for a pleasant ridge walk before coming down into Gotham village for our lunch stop.

Having satisfied the inner person, we re-ascend Gotham Hill, pausing briefly at the summit to enjoy the rearward view before continuing on our way. In contrast to the dizzy heights of Gotham Hill, the area to the north and east is flat, and the path to Clifton takes us over a vast, level plain. As we approach the end of our walk, we can savour the beauties of Clifton village, and, if we wish, complete an optional extension through the celebrated Clifton Grove and back along the riverside.

The Cuckoo Bush Inn, on Leake Road, Gotham, takes its name from the most celebrated of the village's merry tales – that of the local men who fenced in the cuckoo so that he would sing to them all the year round. This is a Punch Taverns house dating back about 150 years. Attractive and traditional, the décor incorporates a delightful clutter of brass and bric-a-brac. Families are welcome, well-behaved dogs also, and there is an outside drinking area. The opening hours are from 12 noon until 3 pm and 5 pm until 11pm, Monday to Friday, and all day (12 noon until 11 pm) on Saturday and Sunday. Food is served every day between 12 noon and 2 pm, and also – on Thursday and Friday evenings only – between 5.30 pm and 8 pm. Lunch is available every day and specialities of the house include chicken curry, Cumberland sausage, sirloin steak and pasta and Stilton bake. Vegetarians are also catered for and there is a choice selection of sandwiches, salads and omelettes. Daily specials are posted on the bar blackboard. Real ales include Bass Pedigree.

> **Telephone**: *0115 983 0306*
> *Refreshments can also be obtained at the* **Sun Inn**, *on The Square in Gotham, any evening, or at lunchtime between Thursday and Sunday (telephone: 0115 983 0484); or at the* **Crusader Inn**, *on the A453 roundabout at Clifton village, towards the end of the walk (telephone: 0115 984 4534). If, alternatively, you favour the alfresco option, you will find a suitable picnic spot by the riverside, just outside Thrumpton.*

 *The Walk*

① Leaving the car park, bear right from **Holgate** to follow the adjacent gated lane down to the riverside. Keep with the track as it bends left, continuing left again at a junction, through a pedestrian access, to follow the **River Trent Greenway**. This delightful path passes **Holme Pit**, now landscaped and incorporating fishing points and wildfowl. Cross an intervening track and continue beside the fields below **Burrows Farm** (where this erstwhile tenderfoot endured his initiation into the rigours of Scout camp). The way continues as an enclosed track beside **Brands Hill Wood**. When I came here in early April, the gorse and blackthorn were in flower, and woodpeckers were drilling holes in the trees. The track bears right onto open fields on the approach to **Barton in Fabis**. The name, I am told, means Barton in the Beans. Join the road, turning right and continuing past the church. Turn right again at **Rectory Place**, then left again by a stile. (2 miles)

Barton and Thrumpton, a couple of miles further on, are traditional farming villages sandwiched between the River Trent and the busy M1 link road. You may yet find true peace along their quiet ways – as you still can around pretty Clifton village, despite some modern housing.

② Follow the clear field path, with **Ratcliffe on Soar power station** visible ahead. The way is clear throughout, although the path at one point passes round three sides of a square to negotiate the edge of one field. Just outside **Thrumpton**, the path joins the riverside, and a useful picnic spot. Follow the farm lane into **Thrumpton** village.

The Hall – a former home of Lord Byron – is not usually open to the public, but the grounds are sometimes the venue for an Easter Fair. Follow the road past the church; pausing perhaps to see the interesting war memorial on the outer (north) wall. This depicts a recumbent soldier, and was put in place to commemorate three local men who fell in the First World War. Continue along the road out of the village, turning left at the T-junction. (2¼ miles)

③ Turn right on reaching a side lane giving access to a bridge over the A453. Continue round to the right; then left at the next turning, resuming the line of the village

THE CUCKOO BUSH INN AT GOTHAM

11

street. Climb up through **Gotham Hill Wood** to arrive at **Cottager's Hill** and Stonepit Wood Scout Camp. Turn left at the guidepost, following the edge of the woods. Continue beside the woods in the second field until you reach a four-way guidepost. Turn right here, using as your waymark a wood which peeps over the hill ahead. Continue over a stile and down the track to a hand-gate on the right. Follow the edge of the field down to the **Railway Walk** (a former mineral track, now converted to a recreational path). Turn left here, and right at the end, continuing along the road to reach the Cuckoo Bush. (2 miles)

'Three Wise Men of Gotham went to sea in a bowl.
If the bowl had been stronger, my tale would have been longer.'
(Anon)

I have a soft spot for Gotham – which some might say is appropriate. My family lived here for a spell, while I was still no more than a twinkle in my daddy's eye; apart from which I have, in the intervening years, spent many a happy hour camping up on Cottager's Hill. It is a village as different from Barton and Thrumpton as chalk from cheese, but it is a village with character, not to mention a long tradition of gypsum mining and

some nice hill paths; and that legend, of the wise men – yes, they really were wise – who decided that they could manage without a royal house in the neighbourhood, and so conspired to convince the king's men that they were all fools.

④ Retrace your steps along **Nottingham Road**, passing the **Kegworth** turning and continuing ahead on reaching the bend by the British Legion headquarters. Keep on past the **Railway Walk**, and on up the hill. Where the track bears left, pass through the gate and turn sharp right up the hillside, veering right again to ascend more steeply and reach **Long Spinney** – where a welcome seat provides an excellent excuse to pause and admire the view back over **Gotham** and towards the Leicestershire border. Pass through the nearby bridle gate and continue, initially beside the wood. Descend easily with the path, crossing a stile to the right of a riding stables entrance and descending to the road. (1 mile)

⑤ Cross over and turn left, looking out for a guidepost on your right. Access the footpath via the ditch board and head left over the fields, making for a distant block of woodland. You should aim initially for the centre of the wood, your first objective being a footbridge to the right of the first electricity pylon.

Two more footbridges follow, roughly on the line of the pylons, after which you should line up with the wood's left-hand edge. Beyond this point, the footpath is much clearer, continuing straight ahead over **Clifton Pasture** to reach the road at the edge of the **Clifton** Council housing estate.

Clifton Pasture used to be acknowledged officially as the biggest field in England. I do not know whether that distinction still applies, a lot of ancient hedgerows up and down the country having, in the cause of 'greater productivity', been grubbed out in the interim. Whatever the truth, this whole vast tract of land, which includes the Barton and Ruddington Moors, remains as we always remember it – a broad, open, low level plain, dissected by the Fairham Brook and with no man-made structures to impede the view other than the old Great Northern Railway line.

Rejoining the road, continue ahead past the **Crusader Inn** and the **Man of Trent**, to reach **Clifton village green**. A quiet side path to the left of the green leads to **Nethergate**. Turn right here, continuing ahead along **Holgate** to reach the car park. (2³/₄ miles)

Clifton village remains a charming backwater, with some peaceful areas, despite a fair amount of development having taken place in the past 50 years or so. A clear distinction has been maintained between new housing and the village environs and a visit to the famous Clifton Grove can still be enjoyed.

⑤ⓐ (optional extension) Follow a footpath to the right of the car park, which leads into **Clifton Grove**. This broad green hilltop ride originally formed an access drive to **Clifton Hall**. The original avenue of elms was destroyed by Dutch elm disease some years ago, but has now been replaced by chestnut trees. After about 1 mile the path descends to join the riverside path. Double back here along the riverside to rejoin the main route at the foot of the gated lane. (2 miles)

Date walk completed:

WEST LEAKE AND THE SOAR VALLEY

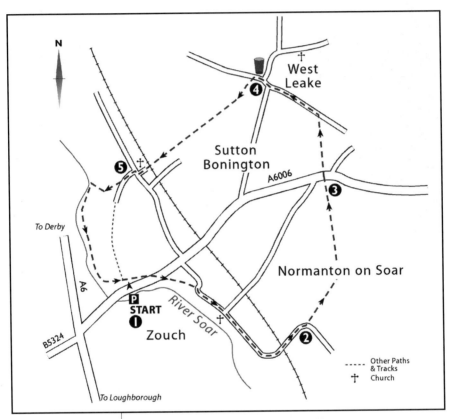

Distance:
8 miles

Starting point:
Public car park,
Zouch, near
Loughborough.
(Grid reference:
SK 504233)

Maps: OS Landranger 129 (Nottingham and Loughborough)
OS Explorer 246 (Loughborough/Melton Mowbray)

How to get there: *From the A60 (Rempstone crossroads)
turn west to follow the A6006 for 5 to 6 miles. The hamlet
of Zouch is the first settlement you come to; it is on the
Leicestershire border after crossing the canal bridge. The
car park is a little way along, on the left, opposite a
footpath guidepost.*

THE PEACEFUL VILLAGE OF NORMANTON ON SOAR

*O*ur walk begins with a short stroll along a section of the 'Zouch Cut'. After meeting the road by the canal bridge, we continue over the fields to Normanton on Soar – just one of several Normantons in Nottinghamshire. This quiet south-western corner of the county contains a number of attractive villages, of varying size and importance, and as well as Normanton we pass through two more in the course of the walk. For the next two and a half miles or so, we cross open country, with little to break the pattern apart from a single isolated farm. After refreshing ourselves at one of the county's most welcoming country pubs, on the outskirts of the pretty hamlet of West Leake, we continue over more field paths to Sutton Bonington. The final stretch of the way follows the gentle River Soar, before returning to the Zouch Cut.

The Star Inn, on Melton Lane, West Leake, is just about as perfect a traditional pub as you could wish to find. There is a ready welcome here, with a cheerful atmosphere and friendly, obliging and smiling service. There used to be a cockpit on the site in less compassionate times, which accounts for its alternative local name of the Leake Pit House. This is an Enterprise Inns house, and has been a pub for over 250 years. The cosy little bar area has real atmosphere, with crooked beams overhead, a tiled floor beneath the feet, and pewter tankards on the shelf. Food is available every lunchtime, and evenings from Tuesday to Saturday. The menu is comprehensive, catering for all tastes including vegetarians and children – and there is even a range of authentic Indian cuisine. If, of course, like me, you prefer something simpler and more traditional, you could try one of the lighter bites – such as a scrumptious hot bacon bap! Real ales include Gibbs Mew.

Telephone: *01509 852 233*
Alternative refreshment facilities will be found at the **Rose and Crown**, *Zouch (telephone: 01509 842 240); the* **Plough**, *Normanton (telephone: 01509 842 228); the* **King's Head**, *Sutton Bonington (telephone: 01509 672 331).*

 *The Walk*

① Leaving the car park, cross the road, passing through the bridleway gate and continuing over the field to reach, and cross, a bridge over the **Zouch Cut**. Turn right and follow the towpath to the junction with the A6002 road. (You could, of course, save a little time and walking distance by omitting this section and sticking to the road. But that, if you don't mind my saying so, would be silly. The saving is negligible, and the peace and beauty of the field and canal side are infinitely preferable to the clamour of the traffic on the road.)

Zouch is situated slap-bang on the county boundary of Nottinghamshire and Leicestershire, and a stranger may well be confused as to which county 'owns' the village. In fact, the River Soar forms the county boundary; hence the hamlet is definitely in Nottinghamshire – unlike its namesake, Ashby de la Zouch, which is in Leicestershire. The locals, by the way, call it 'Zotch'. There is not much to Zouch: a pub, a garage, the river and the 'cut' – and the former mill, now converted to flats. But it provides a gateway to a lovely stretch of peaceful waterside meadowland.

On rejoining the road, cross over and turn left, following the road as far as a footpath sign on the right. Cross the fields on a diagonal line to reach the village of **Normanton on Soar** (and **Main Street**).

A tidy village, Normanton boasts a 17th century manor house which used, at one time, to host garden parties said to rival those at Buckingham Palace. There is also a timber-framed cottage of cruck construction, dating back to the mid-15th century, which is a popular subject with painters. A peaceful village, off the beaten track, Normanton is so quiet that the tread of a passing stranger is enough to set the dogs barking!

Follow **Main Street** through the village, continuing on round a bend and over the railway to reach a second bend; this time to the right. (2 miles)

② Leave the road here, continuing straight on with the hedge on your left as you follow the field boundary. On reaching **Normanton Grange Farm**, skirt carefully around to the right of the buildings, following the arrow waymarks and bearing right a little to continue, still alongside the field boundaries, to **Limekiln Plantation**. Pass through

THE STAR INN AT WEST LEAKE

this attractive wood to reach, and cross, the **A6006** road. (1½ miles)

③ Continue ahead, still following the bridleway, initially with the hedge on your left. Turn left at **Brickyard Lane**, keeping straight on as far as the junction with **Melton Lane** – close to the **Star Inn**. (1¼ miles)

West Leake lies close to the Kingston Brook and, small though it is, has a long history. It was mentioned in Domesday Book as 'Leche', but there is evidence that there was already a settlement here in Roman times. The church is modest but attractive, and there is an old manor house, with remains of fishponds nearby.

We come across some puzzling nomenclature in this vicinity. A Limekiln Plantation with no lime kiln; a Brickyard Lane and a Brickyard Plantation but, so it appears, no brickyard; a Melton Lane many miles from Melton Mowbray; and a Trowell Lane.

Trowell Lane – now there is a conundrum! The spelling suggests that it once led to Trowell, near Wollaton. But that Trowell is a little place, about nine miles away, on the other side of the Trent, with the only possible direct access via a (now-defunct) ferry. Mull that one over while you enjoy your pint!

④ Over the road from **the Star**, cross a stile and bear right to follow the edge of this first field. Keep on, maintaining a diagonal line over several more fields to reach and cross a footbridge. Follow this new line along the ditch side until you reach a guidepost; then turn half-right, crossing the ditch as directed and keeping on over one large field, after which the path continues along the right-hand field boundary.

After crossing a stile, bear left over the fields, crossing two intervening metalled access roads to reach and cross a bridge over the railway and, after passing through the churchyard, continue down **St Anne's Lane** to **Sutton Bonington**. (1½ miles)

Sutton Bonington is really two settlements rolled into one; there are no prizes for guessing their original names. A pleasant linear village, it is the home of the University of Nottingham College of Agriculture, and was also, in earlier days, a centre for the framework knitting industry. Buildings of special interest here include the parish church of St Anne and a fine old mansion dating back to Queen Anne's time. Then there is 'Hobgoblins', a large stone house suspected of being some 300 years old and firmly believed locally to be haunted. A rumour that the house is connected to the parish church via a secret tunnel is, perhaps, less reliable.

⑤ Leaving **St Anne's Lane**, turn right; then left again at **Pasture Lane**. You can, if you wish, save about 1/2 mile by following the lane and its succeeding footpath all the way back to the car park; but resist the temptation, taking instead a footpath on the right, a little way along the lane, and following it down the length of the field. At the far end of the field, go through the gate and turn right, continuing to '**Devil's Elbow**' on the **River Soar**. Turn left here and follow the riverside path back to the **Zouch Cut**.

The River Soar follows the Nottinghamshire/Leicestershire county boundary from just outside Loughborough to its confluence with the Trent at Red Hill, opposite Trent Lock. There is usually plenty of traffic – narrow boats, cabin cruisers, rowing boats and canoes – along the river to enrich your enjoyment, but this is

still a quiet, peaceful stretch of riverside on which to bring a satisfying walk to a beautiful, perfect climax.

When I was a lot younger than I am now, the River Soar was one of those delightful places where we – and many families like ours – used to come on Bank Holiday afternoons to picnic and fish for tiddlers. A rare treat in those far off days when youngsters were, perhaps, satisfied with simpler pleasures than are today's generation. Or am I being unjust?

As a final diversion, if you are very lucky, you might also be able to watch while the entrance lock is put through its paces for the benefit of a passing cabin cruiser or narrowboat.

A short stroll alongside the cut will bring you back to the bridge – and a final field to cross to the car park. (1 3/4 miles)

Date walk completed:

WYSALL, WILLOUGHBY AND THE MIDSHIRES WAY

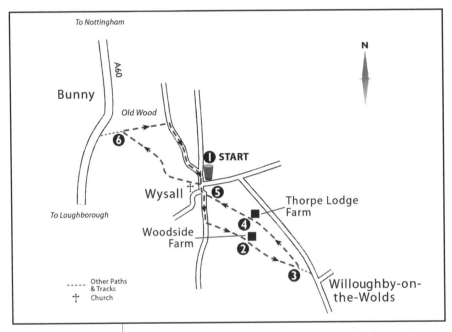

Distance:
7¹/₂ miles

Starting point:
Plough Inn car park, Wysall. (Grid reference: SK 605274). Those not visiting the pub should be able to find ample roadside parking space along the village street.

Maps: OS Landranger 129 (Nottingham and Loughborough) OS Explorer 246 (Loughborough)

How to get there: *From Nottingham (Trent Bridge), follow the Loughborough road (A60) south, crossing the A52 ring road and continuing past Ruddington. Leave the main road at Bradmore, taking the Keyworth road (Pendock Lane), and bending right at a junction of roads to arrive at Wysall village. The Plough Inn is at the beginning of the village, on the left, with its car park opposite.*

GOATS ON THE MOVE AT THORPE IN THE GLEBE

*T*here are five points of special interest on this walk. The first is the parish of Thorpe in the Glebe, which, although consisting today of little more than a scattering of farms, still merits a signboard on the Wymeswold road. Then, just off our route, there is the village of Willoughby-on-the-Wolds, where was fought the last Civil War battle in Nottinghamshire. From here to Bunny Old Woods we follow a section of the Midshires Way; a recreational footpath linking the Ridgeway Path in the south and the Trans-Pennine Trail in the north. And Bunny Old Woods themselves have long been renowned for the bluebells that still flower there in the spring. That makes four special features. And the fifth? Why, the pub in pretty Wysall village, of course; so unmissable that we have provided no fewer than three opportunities to call in! This is a 'figure of eight' ramble, the idea being that you follow one route to Willoughby and another back to Wysall; then you cross the road and follow the same procedure to and from Bunny Old Woods. Well, it adds variety! In essence, there are six sections, four of which follow field paths throughout.

The Plough Inn on Wysall's Main Street is one of my favourite pubs. It could be the fact that I am something of a traditionalist, for there is no inn more traditional than the Plough. Dating back to the 16th century, this lovely old free house stands in an elevated position right at the northern entrance to the village. The outward appearance – white painted frontage, old plough over the door, tables outside in the pretty garden area – all combine to draw one in. And having entered, the flagstoned floors, cosy open fireplace, the clean lines of the timber-faced bar counter and those inevitable little rural touches reinforce the homeliness of the place. The pleasant welcome and the cheerful demeanour of staff and customers alike completes the perfect picture.

There are no special facilities here for children, but families (though not dogs) are welcome at lunchtimes. The pub is open all day and every day, food being served, from a full menu, between 12.30 pm and 2.30 pm, every day except Sunday. Specialities include fresh fish, lasagne, steak and ale pie, curries, salads and ribeye steaks. Hot baguettes and rolls are also available every day, including Sunday. Real ales include Speckled Hen and Landlord's Pride, as well as two guest ales.

Telephone: *01509 880339*

The Walk

① Follow **Main Street** through the village, turning left on the bend by the church to continue along **Wymeswold Road**, After crossing the road bridge at **Kingston Brook**, take the waymarked footpath on the left, following the **Brooklea Farm** road. As you approach the farm, branch off right, still following the waymarked path, and cross two fields diagonally. Turn left along the hedge in the next field. From here the line of the path changes across four successive fields: diagonal – hedge left – diagonal –

diagonal, before crossing a rough area by **Woodside Farm**. (1¼ miles)

The whole of these first two stages of the walk lie within the civil parish of Thorpe in the Glebe. The medieval village, which lay ¹/₂ mile to the south of our route, has long disappeared, but its site is immortalised in the name of Church Site Farm.

② Keep straight on across this large field, following the overhead power line and making for the left-hand end of a wood, where there is a gate and stile. Continue beside the wood, bearing right at the end to

22

cross another stile and turn left, now following the right-hand side of the hedge. Pass through the hedge again as you approach **Triangle Plantation**, keeping to the woodside track through a field gate and on. After the third gate, turn left and follow the hedge down, passing through yet another gate and over the succeeding field on a diagonal line and continuing over the fields from here until you reach a water trough. Turn left now, following a short green lane through the gap. (1 mile)

Although we do not actually visit Willoughby-on-the-Wolds, we are, *at this point, within shouting distance of the village. Inside the church here is the last resting place of Colonel Michael Stanhope, of Shelford, one of those slain at the Battle of Willoughby Field, which was fought here in July 1648. It is said that the villagers climbed the tower to watch the proceedings in a nearby field – although some have suggested that the actual field of battle was rather nearer to the Fosse Way.*

The Midshires Way was opened in 1994 to provide a direct link between the existing Ridgeway route and the proposed

THE PLOUGH INN, WYSALL

Trans-Pennine Trail. In its course, the way crosses five counties, plus Stockport Metropolitan Borough, a distance in total of over 200 miles. It first enters Nottinghamshire between Old Dalby and Willoughby, from where it crosses the south of the county, before finally leaving us again at Kegworth. Because the route is intended as a multiple use way, appropriate roadway diversions are provided for horse riders in those places where the alternative is a basic footpath. You and I, of course, are free to follow either route!

③ Turn left through the gap, now following the **Midshires Way**. The initial stages of this part of the walk cross a series of fields and two incidental farm lanes. (The path follows a pretty straight line as far as the second farm lane, and the waymarking is generally satisfactory, so you should be able to proceed without difficulty up to this point. However, there is scant evidence in places of regular footpath use and some careful navigation may be called for. One point you will need to watch, all the way through to **Wysall,** is the condition of the stiles. At the end of August 2003, most of these were satisfactory and some were in excellent condition. A few, however, were in need of repair.) Soon after crossing the second farm lane, look out for a footbridge over

to your left. Turn right after crossing it, passing through a gap in the hedge. The path crosses straight over this large field to reach, and pass, the extreme right-hand corner of a wood, continuing on at an angle of more or less 45 degrees from the wood, to cross the hedge just to the left of **Thorpe Lodge Farm**. (1 mile)

④ Follow the sequence of hedges round to the right to reach a multiple crossing (two stiles and a footbridge) over the **Kingston Brook**. Bear left then to reach another multiple crossing and continue over the 'ridge and furrow'. Follow the right-hand side of the hedge for the full length of the next field, turning right at the end to reach and cross the next stile. Then bear right a little to reach the top corner of the field and continue through to **Wysall**, turning right along **Main Street**. (1 mile)

Wysall, a typical English village, is a friendly, welcoming place, attractive and quiet, with the two most important buildings – the church and the pub – at opposite ends.

⑤ Cross the road, leaving via an enclosed footpath on the left, identified by the **'Midshires Way'** sign. Go over a stile at the top end of the path, cross the field diagonally, continuing on the left of the hedge over the next two fields. The view from here, over the fields to your left, extends as far as **Charnwood Forest**. Cut through the hedge at the top of this second field, continuing in the same direction along the facing farm track. Go through the hedge again at the top of this field and turn right, still following the hedge. Continue on into the next field, keeping straight ahead where the hedge bends right. Veer left in the next field to cross this and the next, very big one and reach a stile in the extreme top corner, leading into **Bunny Old Wood**. (1¹/₂ miles)

It used to be a common sight in the spring to see young, energetic cyclists speeding down Wilford Hill towards Nottingham with great bundles of bluebells – freshly picked in Bunny Woods – strapped to their rear carriers. The practice is not permitted nowadays of

course, which is a good thing. The proper place to enjoy bluebells – or any other wild flowers – is in their natural habitat. In any case, Bunny Old Wood today is a nature reserve, under the care of the Nottinghamshire Wildlife Trust, so that is another unarguable reason for leaving the bluebells where they are. Just come along in May and enjoy them!

⑥ Cross the stile and follow the path down to join the main east/west track at the bottom, and turn right. Turn right again at the **Wysall** road, which here doubles as the **'equestrian' Midshires Way**, following the road back to **Wysall**. This is not a busy road, and there is a good wide grass verge for most of the way back to the village. (1³/₄ miles)

Date walk completed:

GRANTHAM CANAL, COTGRAVE AND THE VALE OF BELVOIR

VIMY RIDGE FARM, KINOULTON

Distance:
11 miles

Starting point:
Mackley's Bridge,
Kinoulton.
(Grid reference:
SK 679324)

Maps: OS Landranger 129 (Nottingham and Loughborough)
OS Explorer 260 (Nottingham and the Vale of Belvoir)

How to get there: *From Gamston, on the Nottingham ring road, follow the A52 east as far as the Holme House traffic lights, turning right here onto Stragglethorpe Road. After crossing the Fosse Way, continue to Cropwell Bishop and turn right at Kinoulton Road. Mackley's Bridge car park is 2¹/₂ miles further on, on the left beside the canal.*

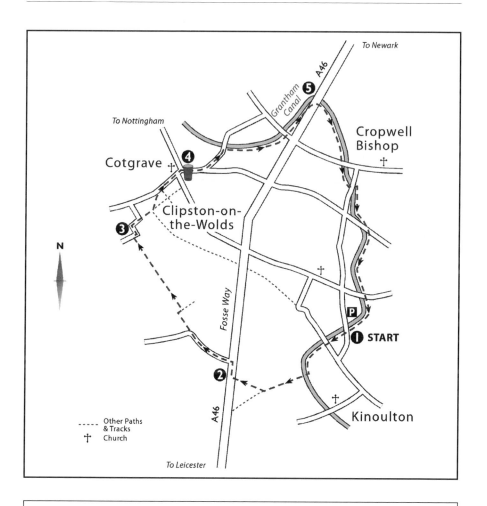

*W*e start the walk with our feet planted firmly inside the Vale of Belvoir, the traditional home of Stilton cheese (and the Dukes of Rutland). Soon after starting, we pass close to a farm – now derelict – with a name and history that recall one of the bitterest campaigns of the First World War. After crossing the Fosse Way, we walk through the forest lands of Cotgrave Wolds to reach the former mining village of Cotgrave, before rejoining the Grantham Canal for a gentle saunter back to our starting point.

The Manvers Arms – a Pub Estates house – stands right in the heart of Cotgrave, opposite the church and on the junction of the three main routes in and out of the village. Built in about 1725, it was formerly a coaching inn – a history still recognisable in the ancient timbers, and the general décor of the lounge and dining areas. Families are welcome; so also are dogs (but only in the tap room), if they are well behaved. The pub is open all day and every day, with food served at lunchtime from Tuesday to Sunday, and in the evening from Tuesday to Thursday. Specialities include 8-ounce rump steaks, large Yorkshire puddings with a choice of savoury fillings, home-made pies and all-day breakfasts. A separate children's menu is also available, and those at the opposite end of the age range can get a full meal (including tea or coffee) between 12 noon and 3 pm on Tuesday, Wednesday and Thursday, all at very reasonable cost. A traditional roast is served on Sundays, also at an attractive price.

Telephone: *0115 989 2293 or 0115 989 4888*
Grannie's Tea Room *at 3 Bingham Road, Cotgrave is also highly recommended for quick, friendly service and a wide variety of light meals and snacks at reasonable cost (telephone: 0115 989 4461).*

 *The Walk*

There is no bridge today at Mackley's Bridge, and very few elsewhere on the Grantham Canal, though the designation survives. The canal was closed many years ago and most of the hump-backed bridges removed. If and when the dreams of the Grantham Canal Restoration Society come to fruition, this may all change.

① Cross the road and follow the towpath, going in a south-westerly direction. Here on the western fringe of the Vale, the countryside is gentle and peaceful, with the level, arable fields giving place ahead to the low, wooded hills of the **Cotgrave Wolds.**

This is one stretch of canal which normally carries a good depth of water, with plenty of wildfowl to add charm to the journey.

After crossing the road at **Wild's Bridge**, bend left with the canal at **Devil's Elbow** before turning right over **Irish Jack's Bridge** to follow the track past **Vimy Ridge Farm.**

Vimy Ridge Farm was so named by Sir Jesse Hind, a prominent Nottingham solicitor, whose son

Monty lost his life at Vimy Ridge during the 1914-18 war. During the Depression of the inter-war years, Sir Jesse employed many sons of ex-servicemen here at Vimy Ridge. The avenue of poplar trees which he planted to commemorate the fallen, being now in a dangerous condition, is itself under sentence of death, but, happily, scheduled for replacement. The farm buildings, meanwhile, stand derelict and forlorn, reflecting perhaps the scene at that other Vimy Ridge some 80 to 90 years ago.

As the track ascends beyond the farm, pause awhile to enjoy the backward view over the **Vale of Belvoir.** If conditions are favourable you should be able to make out

Belvoir Castle, the seat of the Dukes of Rutland, on the far side of the Vale at the extreme end of its wooded ridge. Continue along the track, turning right along the outer edge of **Kinoulton Gorse.** Turn briefly left at the far end of the wood, then right again, continuing with the hedge on your right to reach the **Fosse Way** (the **A46**) and turn right onto it. (2 miles)

Two thousand years ago, or thereabouts, the Romans came and built a road across the Vale of Belvoir. The Fosse Way, unlike the Vale's other engineering features, the Grantham Canal and the Cotgrave Colliery, has survived in use and developed far beyond the dreams of Caesar's hordes, so the rambler of today needs to be

THE MANVERS ARMS IN THE CENTRE OF COTGRAVE

pretty spry to avoid extermination by the modern motoring legions!

② After passing **Owthorpe Lodge**, cross the road to take the first turning on the left (**Laming Gap Lane**). The **Fosse Way** here is a single carriageway road, very straight and fast, so great care is demanded in the crossing thereof. Follow this side road for about 3/4 mile, passing **Wynnstay Wood**. Keep straight on where the road bends, entering **Cotgrave Forest** and staying with the main track as it bends right and left, to reach the hamlet of **Clipston**. (2¹/₂ miles)

③ Continue forward along the village street as far as the second bend. Leave the road here, following the rough track on the right past **Boot Pit Plantation** and emerging onto the fields. There are more splendid views here, over **Cotgrave** village, and, to the left, across the **Trent Valley** and the city of **Nottingham**. Follow the path left and right around the field margins, before branching off left to continue to the road. Turn right then for **Cotgrave**, and the **Manvers Arms**. (1¹/₄ miles)

Fifty years or so ago Cotgrave was just a typical agricultural village. Then they discovered a seam of coal. A shaft was sunk, houses built, and immigrants from the northern coalfields welcomed in to supplement the local labour force. And Cotgrave Colliery was in business. Now, the wheel has turned full circle. The colliery is gone, its site occupied by a country park. That might, in some respects, be considered an improvement – not everyone welcomed the sinking of a coal mine in our green and pleasant neighbourhood. All the same, Cotgrave Colliery represented a phase, albeit brief, in the history and development of my home territory. And there is something sad about the decline of an industry which once supported a vibrant, hard-working community.

④ Leave **Cotgrave** via **Bingham Road** and **Hollygate Lane,** turning right onto the canal towpath at **Hollygate Bridge.** Most of this stretch of the canal is dry and overgrown, but the track is firm and the walking pleasant and gentle. Runners and cyclists also use the towpath; so keep your ears open for the sound of trainers or tyres disturbing the gravel surface as they approach from behind.

Cross the road at **Mann's Bridge** and continue to **Fosse Bridge**, one of the few surviving bridges on Nottinghamshire's share of the canal – which means we are this time saved the bother of dodging the traffic and can safely pass under the roadway. And the bonus? A pleasant picnic area whereat to rest and reflect! (2 miles)

The Grantham Canal was opened in 1797, providing a link between the River Trent at Nottingham and the Lincolnshire town of Grantham, a distance of 33 miles. As with so many other canals, trade was adversely affected by the coming of the railways in the 19th century, but the canal managed to survive until 1929. Those sections that were still in water then remained popular with anglers, and the towpath was also in regular use. I made a vow, a long time ago, at some time to walk the full distance. I did it – many years later! Today, much of the canal is dry and overgrown. But it still harbours its share of fish and fowl. And the towpath, as we have seen, is still a popular pedestrian freeway.

One feature of the old canal that still remains and is maintained is the regular distance posts indicating the mileage from the River Trent. They provide a useful guide to how much farther you have to travel. Just for the record, Mackley's Bridge is 10$\frac{1}{4}$ miles from the river.

⑤ The canal bed is still dry, but less overgrown, as we resume our walk; it is more a green trough here, where the banks have eroded and the original bed filled in over the years. The view over the former canal and the adjacent fields to **Hoe Hill Wood** is very pleasant, and it is easy to visualise the prettiness of the scene as it must have been when there was water in the canal, and some natural and commercial life on the water. Cross **Nottingham Road** (which leads into **Cropwell Bishop**) and continue to **Kinoulton Road,** which is crossed obliquely. An inscription on the crossing here – easily missed – tells us that this was **Roving Bridge.** Continue past **Cropwell Bishop Wharf** to **Colston Bridge,** bearing left a shade at the road to regain access to the canal path. Soon after **Spencer's Bridge** – the last road crossing – a pretty little tree-girt spot with a rustic seat, a footbridge (of doubtful solidity!) and a modicum of water invites us to rest awhile. A little late in the day, perhaps, with less than half a mile to go – but who's counting? When you have enjoyed your rest, continue along the towpath until you very soon reach **Mackley's Bridge**. (3$\frac{1}{4}$ miles)

 *Date walk completed:*

LAKES AND WATERWAYS AROUND HOLME PIERREPONT

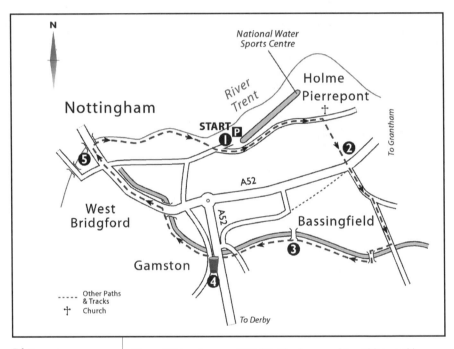

Distance:
10 miles

Starting point:
National Water
Sports Centre,
Holme Pierrepont.
(Grid reference:
SK 610389)

Maps: OS Landranger 129 (Nottingham and Loughborough)
OS Explorer 260 (Nottingham/Vale of Belvoir)

How to get there: *From Nottingham (Trent Bridge),
follow the Radcliffe Road (A6520/6011) out of town,
turning left after Gamston Bridge onto Regatta Way.
Continue round a right-hand bend and bear left where the
road branches for the Water Sports Centre and Country
Park. There is a large public parking area here. Parking is
also available en route: by the canal at Cotgrave Bridge
(639367) and at Tollerton Bridge (608368)*

SKYLARKS NATURE RESERVE

*T*his walk tours the cream of the South Nottinghamshire waterways, starting with the most impressive feature of them all, the National Water Sports Centre. As we continue, we wander through Rushcliffe's own miniature Lakeland – the nomenclature of which is later reflected in the road system of our newest local housing development. The circuit is rounded off by a saunter along the banks of a once busy canal – still alive but resting – and those of our own world-renowned river, the Trent.

The Goose, on Ambleside at Gamston, is an ultra-modern Hardy and Hanson house situated between the Nottingham outer ring road (A52) and Gamston's equally modern executive housing development. A Family Food House, opened as recently as 1998, it cannot yet claim any special historical interest. (I have lived all my life within a coupe of miles of Gamston, but am unaware of any special significance in the pub's name!) But history is, after all, of secondary importance to the obvious attractions, liquid and solid, of the place. The Goose stands in an enviable position, drawing its clientele from

33

the estate on the one hand and the commuter traffic on the other – not to mention the occasional passing rambler. Every desirable facility is here: a family room, children's play area, and outdoor and non-smoking areas. Dogs are welcome outside or – in the case only of guide dogs for the blind or deaf – indoors. The pub is open all day, every day, from 11 am (12 noon on Sunday) and food is likewise available until 10 pm (9 pm on Sundays). The menu is impressive, and caters for all tastes. But does not appear to include roast goose!

Telephone: *0115 982 1041*
Alternative refreshment facilities are available at **Shepherds' Brewer's Fayre** *at Stragglethorpe (telephone 0115 933 3337); in season, at the* **Waterside Café**, *in the country park, where there is also a picnic area. Picnicking is also possible at Skinner's Lock, on the canal.*

 *The Walk*

① Follow the access road back from the car park to **Adbolton Lane** and turn sharp left, following the lane to **Holme Pierrepont** and passing, in turn, the **Buggyland Quad Park**, a racing circuit for four-wheeled motor bikes (a contradiction in terms, but you know what I mean), a water-ski training site and cableway, and the **Skylarks Nature Reserve**.

The Trent Valley has been heavily scarred over the years by the excavations of the sand and gravel industries. However, one cannot but applaud the measures that have been taken in recent years to reshape the worked out land. Nowhere is this restoration more evident than around Holme Pierrepont, where a vast acreage of former gravel-land has been converted into a world-class water sports centre set in a country park and offering some of the most comprehensive facilities in the world. Is it too much to hope, perhaps, that it might one day come into its own as an Olympic venue? Other former quarries in the area have been, or are being, converted into delightful areas of nature reserve, parkland, woodland and lakes, admirably complementing the already existent facilities of river and canal.

Some unexpected and interesting results have accrued here from both the quarrying and the subsequent restoration. Quite a few years ago, I seem to remember, a prehistoric dugout canoe was unearthed (or ungravelled?) at Holme Pierrepont. Like the Mary Rose, it had to be dried out very, very slowly to prevent it from disintegrating.

Turn right at **Sandays Corner** – opposite the entrance to **Holme Pierrepont Hall** – and follow **Sandy Lane** through to the **A52** at **Holme House**. Whereas Adbolton Lane has been upgraded in recent years, Sandy Lane has gone into reverse and is now closed to motor traffic, making walking on it more enjoyable. (2¹/₄ miles)

Holme Pierrepont Hall is a fine early Tudor red-brick manor house, which is well worth visiting. Much of the house,

including the ballroom, drawing room and long gallery, has been modernised by the current owners, and the secret courtyard garden is especially recommended. For opening hours and entrance charges, telephone 0115 933 2371.

② Cross the road via the traffic lights, continuing straight on along **Stragglethorpe Road**. Turn right by **Shepherds restaurant** and continue to the **Grantham Canal**. The towpath follows the left side of the canal, but a better, more intimate footpath leads off from the adjacent car park to follow the right-hand bank. This terminates at the restored

THE GOOSE AT GAMSTON

Skinner's Lock, where there is also a picnic area. After crossing the footbridge over the lock, continue along the towpath until you reach a vehicular bridge, where a farm track and footpath lead in from **Bassingfield**, on the right. (2³/₄ miles)

③ Continue along the towpath to **Tollerton Lane**. You can, if you wish, turn right here and follow the road round to the junction with the ring road. But for the slight difference in walking distance involved, I prefer to remain with the canal for now. The important thing to bear in mind, whichever you choose, is that you have to cross the busy road – and the safest place to do so is at the road junction, where you do not need to clamber over any safety barriers! Just take care – and exercise patience in crossing. Over the main road, join **Ambleside** and turn left, to reach **the Goose**. (1 mile)

In the course of our walk so far we have seen and passed a number of lakes – some large, like the two-kilometre rowing course at the Water Sports Centre, some smaller, like the one in the Skylarks Nature Reserve, and those under development beside Sandy Lane. The only lakes at Gamston are the puddles, when it rains. But a few more impressive lakes and tarns – such as Coniston,

Easedale and Elterwater – are commemorated in the local road system. Quite sets the feet itching, it do!

④ Cross over **Ambleside** and rejoin the canal, following the towpath past the rear of the supermarket. This section of the canal has inevitably been suburbanised – but that is not to decry it. It is pleasant walking, and there is rather more wildlife to be seen here – no doubt attracted by the greater availability of food to be provided by the passing populace. The inevitable species of mallard, coot and swan were here of course – and I even spotted that goose at one point! And then there were the ones I didn't see or identify, chattering away nineteen to the dozen somewhere among the reeds.

Pass under **Gamston Bridge**. The road here has been dual carriageway for a number of years, although the bridge has been left intact. Thus the Nottingham-bound lane passes over the bridge, while the outward lane is culverted. So you still have to brave the traffic, but only in half of the crossing. We are now passing through **West Bridgford** and following the main road more closely. I met a number of anglers along here – more, in fact, than I had seen here for many years.

Keep straight forward on reaching the **Trent Boulevard/Holme Road** junction, now following the left of the road, as for **Lady Bay Bridge**. Turn left and follow **Scarrington Road** round as far as the **Environment Agency** entrance and rejoin the canal side, following this through to **Trent Lock** and the river. (2 miles)

When the Midland Railway line between Nottingham and Melton Mowbray was closed, back in the 1960s, the rail bridge over the river was converted to a relief road, linked to the Radcliffe road. This entailed the culverting of a section of the canal – a process that is unlikely ever to be reversed. As a result, any re-vitalisation of the canal will entail the construction of a replacement section somewhere further down-river.

Lady Bay Bridge itself won a moment of fame a few years ago when it was miraculously transported to eastern Europe to star, with Alec Guinness, in the televised adaptation of Tinker, Tailor, Soldier, Spy.

⑤ Turn right at the river, passing under **Lady Bay Bridge**. A lovely, peaceful riverside stroll follows. There are many boats moored alongside the opposite bank, including both cabin cruisers and pleasure cruisers. As you proceed, and the city and its immediate suburbs are left behind, the outlook, particularly over the far side of the river, becomes more rural. Continue back to the **National Water Sports Centre** and **country park**. (2 miles)

Date walk completed:

HOVERINGHAM TO MORTON, AND THE TRENT VALLEY WAY

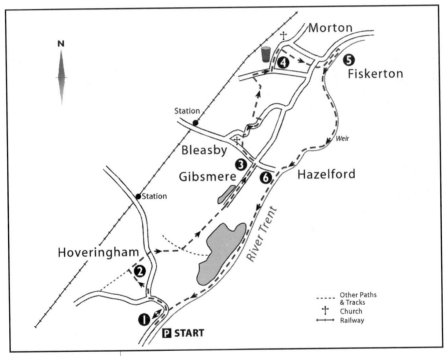

Distance:
10½ miles

Starting point:
Trentside car park,
Hoveringham:
(Grid reference:
SK 701461)

Maps: OS Landranger 120 (Mansfield and Worksop and 129 (Nottingham and Loughborough); OS Explorer 260 (Nottingham/ Vale of Belvoir) and 271 (Newark on Trent).

How to get there: From Nottingham, via the A612 (Southwell road). Turn right immediately beyond the Lowdham roundabout; then left after the railway crossing. Continue through Caythorpe, following the road until it meets the riverside, where there is a large roadside parking area.

GLEBE FARM IS PASSED ON THE ROUTE

*T*his walk could very easily, if we are not careful, degenerate into a glorified pub-crawl, there being four excellent hostelries on the route, and a fifth just a short stroll off it. Better curb your enthusiasm, though – unless you are prepared to snore the afternoon away on the riverbank (which might not be such a bad idea at that!). This is another area with a history of sand and gravel extraction, but the only evidence of quarrying seen along the way nowadays is the scenic beauty of the lakes and ponds left behind, now the preserve of Canada geese and the various angling groups. The villages along the way – Hoveringham, Bleasby, Morton and Fiskerton – remain delightful havens of calm. The walking is easy and gentle, the first half dozen miles along a varied assortment of good paths and tracks, the final four and a half following the Trent Valley Way upstream.

The Full Moon Inn, adapted from a row of cottages on Main Street in the tiny village of Morton, is sheer perfection: a two centuries old traditional village pub with half-timbered interior, beamed ceilings, flag-stoned floors and an open fireplace. It is open Monday to Saturday from 11 am until 3 pm, and between 6 pm and 11 pm each evening, Sunday 12 noon until 3 pm and 7 pm to 10.30 pm Full meals and bar snacks are served daily, and in the evenings, and specialities include chicken tikka masala, salmon fillet, Full Moon Caesar salad, and garlic herb chicken. There are alternative choices for vegetarians and a separate menu for children. Senior citizens are also catered for with a special two-course luncheon available from Monday to Friday. Families are welcome and there is a children's play area as well as an outside terrace. Guide dogs are allowed. Real ales include Speckled Hen, Bombardier and Full Moon Bitter, with a regular change of guest ales.

Telephone: *01636 830 251*
Alternative refreshment facilities will be found at the **Reindeer Inn** *(telephone: 0115 966 3629) and the* **Marquis of Granby** *(telephone: 0115 966 3080), both in Main Street, Hoveringham; or at the* **Bromley Arms** *(telephone: 01636 830 789) on Fiskerton Wharf.*

 *The Walk*

① Follow the road round to the left, then go right at a road junction to reach **Hoveringham** village. When almost opposite the **Marquis of Granby**, turn left along a short access lane, then right again at the end to pass the rear of the **Reindeer Inn**. The Reindeer backs directly onto the village cricket ground – and offers the ideal situation from which to enjoy the play, with picnic tables, and a tiny hatch – the Boundary Bar – whereat to order refreshment. An idyllic spot, as my wife and I have found on occasion, at which to take a rest and a reviver at the end of a strenuous walk! Continue round the boundary and over the ensuing fields to cross a footbridge and turn right onto a bridleway. (1 mile)

The village of Hoveringham gave an identity to Hoveringham Gravels – now part of the Tarmac Group – which in turn gives some idea of the history of the countryside hereabouts. It is still a pleasant, tidy village, though, with plenty of old buildings, and is completely unspoilt by the nearby gravel workings.

② Follow the bridleway for some distance, to where a curving access road leads out to the **Thurgarton** road. Go briefly to the right here, and then left on the bend, rejoining the bridleway, with the wooded high ground of the **Trent Hills** prominent ahead. After passing a footbridge on your right (do not cross it), the track bends left. Cross a gravel lane and a footbridge, continuing through a bridle-gate and on over a very large field. After merging with a rough lane, the way continues ahead with a former gravel pit on the right. A rough parking area here is reserved for members of the Derbyshire (yes, that's right) Angling Club. Pass **Glebe Farm** and continue through **Gibsmere**, a pretty, secluded hamlet with a fishing pond – this one the province of the Nottingham Fly Fishers. Reach a crossroads just outside **Bleasby**, where a seat on the junction offers the opportunity for a brief rest. (2¼ miles)

Bleasby is another of those traditional Nottinghamshire

THE BROMLEY ARMS ON FISKERTON WHARF

villages of red brick and pantile roofs that, though the lifestyle may have undergone a transformation, have changed little in outward appearance. The old industries of farming, framework knitting and shoemaking have declined or disappeared and most of the workforce commutes these days to Nottingham. But history lives on here in the 14th century farmhouse – 'The Old House' – with its notable dovecote, and at the Wagon and Horses pub, dating back to the 17th century. William Booth, the founder of the Salvation Army, spent part of his childhood at Bleasby. And a whipping post was erected here back in 1763 – so watch your step!

③ Turn left, walking towards **Bleasby**. At the entrance to the village, cross a stile on the right and continue over the field, turning left over a second stile and keeping straight on along the left-hand field boundary. Where the path branches, take the rightward option, still following the field boundary, to reach a road, where continue forward. After negotiating a double bend, leave the road at a guidepost on the left, crossing the stile and following the line of the hedge up the field. Turn right over a second stile at the top of the field and continue, still following the hedge

along the right of this long field. Turn left again in the next field, passing a small wood and continuing to a farm road; then turn right. Keep straight forward, ignoring the next junction, to reach the outskirts of **Morton**. Turn left at a Y-junction and continue to the **Full Moon Inn**. (1³/₄ miles)

The little village of Morton is attractive and welcoming, with a long and interesting history. It is, according to reports, a 'sleepy beauty' of a village, where farming folk, businessmen and retired villagers live together in harmony. Small as the community is, there is plenty going on here – and new building has been carefully controlled.

④ Leave **Morton** via a metalled driveway on the right, just past the pub, continuing along a narrow, enclosed path between a pair of houses. Veer left then over a field to follow the hedge-line. The path alternates to right and left of the field boundary to reach the road just short of **Fiskerton**. Turn left and continue into the village, turning right through the **Bromley Arms'** car park to reach **Fiskerton Wharf**. (1 mile)

Just across the river from Fiskerton Wharf is East Stoke, the site, in 1487, of the last battle of the Wars of the Roses. The army of

THE RIVER TRENT

Lambert Simnel, the pretender to the throne of England, forded the river from Fiskerton – probably from this very spot where the Bromley now stands – having marched there from Southwell. Had the pub been in existence five hundred years ago, they might have considered pausing here for long enough to wet their whistles before crossing – and thus, perhaps, have prevented the ensuing bloodbath. The area where the fighting was fiercest is still known as Red Gutter, from the volume of blood that flowed in this marshy trench.

⑤ Turn right at the wharf, following the river upstream. The wharf itself is private ground, but there is a public right of way, provided you stay with the path and keep your dog (if you have one) under control. The same, of course, goes for children, because the drop over the edge into the river is sheer. Beyond the wharf, the riverside field path is joined, and with it the **Trent Valley Way**. This initial stretch from **Fiskerton** follows the top of the flood bank, before straying closer to the river where, for a time, the path is narrow and subject to the encroachment of grass and weeds.

But these are part of the adventure – an occupational hazard along Nottinghamshire's footpaths! The path improves after we pass **Hazelford Lock** and continues to the eponymous ferry. (2 miles)

The Trent Valley Way is one of Nottinghamshire's middle-distance footpaths, and follows the river (more or less) all the way from Trent Lock on the Derbyshire border to West Stockwith in the far north of the county. I say 'more or less' because there are sections where the Way, for one reason or another, strays away from the river for a while. Here, though, it remains faithful to its title!

Hazelford Ferry, like the locks and bridges on the Grantham Canal, exists today as just a name on the map, with nothing tangible to support it. In the days before Hitler's war, Hazelford Ferry was a popular spot for weekend recreation of the masses – as also were Gunthorpe Bridge and Wilford Corner. The popularity of all of these picnic areas has declined today with the increasing affluence and higher aspirations of the grandchildren of those masses.

As a matter of interest, the Ordnance Survey calls it 'Hazelford', while the British Waterways notice here spells it 'Hazleford'. We, just to be different, always called it 'Hazzleford'. So which is right? I suppose, like the man said, you just pays your money and you takes your choice!

⑥ Continuing along the riverside, the path improves immeasurably as it crosses the wide green sward of **Hoveringham Pastures**, flanked here on both sides by water – there is a vast lake on the right and, on the left, the broad stately stream of the **River Trent**, home here to a huge colony of Canada geese. Joining the **Hoveringham** road, continue straight forward, back to the parking area. (2¹/₂ miles)

Date walk completed:

BEATING THE BOUNDS FROM TROWELL TO STRELLEY AND COSSALL

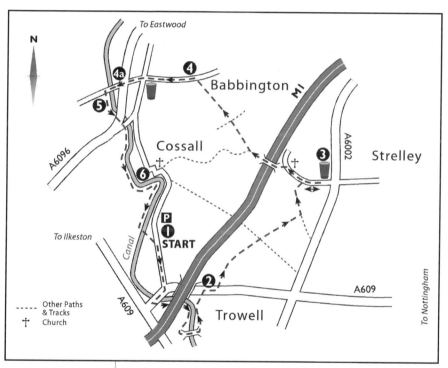

Distance:
9¹/₂ (or 10¹/₂) miles

Starting point: Cossall Road car park, Trowell. (Grid reference: SK 483412)

Maps: OS Landranger 129 (Nottingham and Loughborough)
OS Explorer 260 (Nottingham/Vale of Belvoir)

How to get there: Follow the A609 west from Nottingham, bypassing Wollaton village. After passing under the M1 at Trowell, turn right onto Cossall Road and continue for ³/₄ mile to a canalside car park on the left.

THE VILLAGE OF COSSALL

*W*e start and finish our walk on the towpath of the Nottingham Canal. Much of this section has been filled in and landscaped, while some is relatively dry and overgrown. We pass beneath the M1 motorway, but, happily, it is left behind with remarkable rapidity. Once we are away from it there is genuine beauty and history to be found throughout this little enclave between the boundaries of city and county.

After leaving the canal, we strike across country, following well marked but quiet ways to Strelley village and a first class watering hole at the Broad Oak pub. Appetites satisfied, we cross the motorway bridge to follow some less frequented field paths to Babbington before continuing along quiet byways to Awsworth, where the canal is rejoined. There is more water to be found here, providing a habitat for wildfowl – and anglers.

We leave the canal again, but only briefly, as we ascend to Cossall village, which has a link with a famous local writer and is the site of an unusual war memorial.

The Broad Oak, in Strelley's Main Street, is an attractive and welcoming Hardy Hanson house in a perfect village setting. The inn is about 200 years old and that eponymous broad oak tree dominates the grassy frontal area. The pub is open from 11 am to 11 pm, Monday to Saturday, and between 12 noon and 10.30 pm on Sundays. Food is available daily from opening time until 9 pm, with a comprehensive range of starters and main courses, including fish dishes, pastas, salads and vegetarian items. Those whose needs are lighter may choose from a selection of sandwiches and baguettes, jacket potatoes or burgers. A full traditional lunch is served on Sundays from 12 noon.

Telephone: *0115 929 3340*
Food and drink can also be obtained at the **Gardeners Inn** *on the corner of Westby Lane in Cossall (telephone: 0115 932 3087).*

The Walk

① Join the towpath and turn left. This section of the canal has been filled in for most of the way through to **Trowell**, but one or two ponds remain to add attraction to the broad, tree-lined green way that survives.

In 1951 Trowell was selected as the 'Festival Village' on the grounds that it was a typical English village, albeit an industrial one.
The Nottingham Canal was constructed between 1792 and 1796 to provide a link between the River Trent at Nottingham and the Cromford Canal at Langley Mill, a distance of 14³/₄ miles. It was intended as a rival to the

Erewash Canal, which also terminated at Langley Mill, and which it was feared would place the Nottinghamshire collieries at a disadvantage. The Beeston Canal, also opened in 1796, joining Nottingham Canal at Lenton, thus creating a valuable bypass of the Trent shallows between Clifton Grove and Trent Bridge. The coming of the railways, as we have already noted elsewhere, sounded the death knell of the commercial canal system, and today the only navigable section of the Nottingham Canal is that between Lenton and Trent Bridge, which still, with the Beeston Canal, forms a popular through route for pleasure craft.

Pass, in turn, beneath the A609 and the M1 and rejoin the towpath. This part of the canal, although mostly dry, has not been filled in, but has been designated as a nature reserve by the Broxtowe Borough Council. Cross **Swansea Bridge** – the towpath effectively ends here – and turn sharp left to follow the opposite bank of the canal. Turn right at a guidepost, crossing a stile, and follow the **Bramcote** footpath up the field to reach the road (**A609**). Cross over and turn right. (2½ miles)

② Turn left at **Waterloo Lane**, which doubles as a service access to the **Trowell Motorway Service Area**. There is no public vehicular access, but we, as walkers, are privileged. Where the roadway bends left, pass through the hedge, as directed by the guidepost, and turn left, following the track alongside the field boundary. Keep straight forward at a crossways, passing **Shaw's Plantation** and continuing to a T-junction. Turn left here and carry on to **Strelley** village, turning right to follow the road to the **Broad Oak**. (2 miles)

③ Return through **Strelley** village, passing the church, and continuing to a bridleway sign on the left. Take this turning, and cross the **M1** bridge. Leave this lane via a footpath on the right, turning left in the field to follow its edge. Keep to the right, passing **Turkey Fields Farm** (all the turkeys were geese when I came!) to reach and cross a

stile in the field corner. Cross the next field, and continue through **Spring Wood**. Then go on over the fields to reach a lane by **Strelley Park Farm**. Cross the lane and continue, maintaining the same line over the first field to reach a gate. Cross the stile to the right of the gate; then bear left over the field to reach a stile leading into the next field. Descend this one, with the hedge on your right, bearing left at the bottom to cross a stile leading into a scrubby little wood. Continue on, bearing right to **Babbington House Farm** and passing between a pair of barns to cross a stile and reach **Westby Lane** and turn left. (2 miles)

Babbington today consists of little more than a hall and a farm, and there is little evidence to be seen of the original shallow shafts, which, before 1840, marked the location of the Babbington (later Cinderhill) Colliery. You might, though, while passing through that scrubby wood I mentioned, spot a depression, bounded by a low bank, on your left. This could well be one of the old shafts. (I suppose they are capped. But don't tempt providence.)

④ Follow the road round a double bend to reach **Awsworth**. Cross over here and continue down **Newton's Lane**. Cross the main road (**A6096**) and turn left to reach a side turning and join the canal towpath, travelling south. (1 mile)

④ⓐ For an optional extension: turn right here instead of left, following a footpath for some way till you reach an anglers' car park. Join the towpath here and continue south. This is one of the better stretches of the **Nottingham Canal**, popular with anglers and offering a good view of the impressive **Bennerley Viaduct**. Rejoin the main route at the above point. (1 mile)

Constructed of wrought iron lattice girders, the remarkable Bennerley Viaduct was erected in 1876/77 to carry the Great Northern Railway over the River Erewash and the Erewash and Nottingham Canals.

⑤ The canal here is more true to its designation. Although by no means navigable, there is plenty of water. A heron flapped lazily on his way on my approach, while a swan sitting her nest ignored me completely. And there was no lack of the ubiquitous mallard and coot. A brief diversion by an industrial estate bypasses a former aqueduct before rejoining the canal proper. At a gravel lane, turn left up the hill. Where the track levels out, take the footpath on the left, crossing a field to reach **Cossall** village and turning

THE BROAD OAK AT STRELLEY

49

right for the parish church and **Church Cottage**. (1¹/₄ miles)

Church Cottage, next to the church, was the home of D. H. Lawrence's fiancé, Louie Burrows, and was featured by the author in his novel The Rainbow.

In Cossall churchyard, close to the more conventional, 20th century war memorial, stands a similar monument to three local men who served at Waterloo. John Shaw and Richard Waplington, of the Life Guards, were both killed in the battle; Thomas Wheatley, of the Light Dragoon Guards, returned home and is buried in the churchyard here. It is interesting to see that, although Waterloo happened close on two hundred years ago, somebody still cares enough to place flowers on the memorial.

Jack Shaw, a prize fighter turned cavalryman, is credited with having killed no fewer than eight of the enemy before being overcome by superior numbers. My mother once told me she was descended from Shaw – but whether directly or indirectly I do not know. The vintage had clearly been watered down somewhat before I appeared on the scene.

⑥ Continue left out of the churchyard, following the road left and right down the hill and out of the village. A footpath on the right leads back to a footbridge over the canal. Cross this and turn left, back to the car park. (³/₄ mile)

Date walk completed:

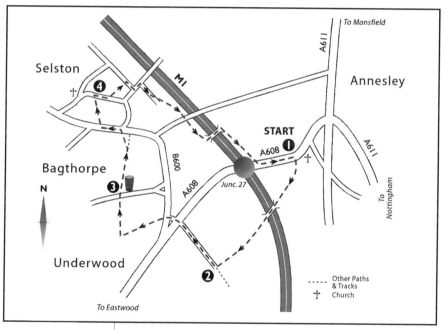

Walk 8

ANNESLEY AND BAGTHORPE, IN THE HEART OF LAWRENCE'S COUNTRY

Distance:
8 (or 8¹/₂ or 9) miles

Starting point: Sherwood Park roundabout, on the A608 east of the M1 (junction 27). (Grid reference: SK 496521)

Maps: OS Landranger 120 (Mansfield and Worksop)
OS Explorer 269 (Chesterfield and Alfreton)

How to get there: From Nottingham: Follow the A611 through Hucknall, turning left onto the A608 at Annesley. From the M1: Leave at junction 27 and join the A611, travelling east. There are lay-bys on both sides of the A608, the one alongside the southern carriageway (westbound) being more spacious, and better.

THE ROUTE AS IT DIPS DOWN TOWARDS FELLEY

*T*his walk starts, to all intents and purposes, virtually on the doorstep of a modern industry – the Kodak works. But that is incidental; the traditional industries, now just a memory, are coal mining and, to a lesser extent, iron founding. This is part of the area described by D. H. Lawrence, who was born at Eastwood, as 'the country of my heart'. The traditional family estates have now declined, but we can still follow the ancient lane through Annesley Park to Felley and Underwood. A devious route takes us on to discover a certain unexpected intimacy in the quiet lanes and paths, old and new communities and green fields around delightful Bagthorpe, with its charming rural pub. From here we cross more fields to 'Inkerman' (suggesting a Crimea connection) and Selston, the final resting place of a gypsy king.

The **Shepherd's Rest**, at Lower Bagthorpe, is an attractive country inn set back from the narrow through lane in this scattered community. A Scottish and Newcastle house, it dates back to around the early 1800s and, in keeping with its age, ghostly sightings have been reported by many of the locals. All those desirable facilities are here – non-smoking zone, outside drinking area, children's play area and family room. Well-behaved dogs are welcome too.

There is all-day opening from 12 noon, and food is served in the week from 12 noon until 3 pm and between 5 pm and 9 pm. Specialities change from week to week, but are likely to include such delicacies as salmon fillet with Hollandaise sauce, half a roast chicken, and sweet and sour pork. There is a choice of baguettes (with salad and chips), and bar snacks are available all day. There is a carvery on Sundays between 12 noon and 3 pm, after which the normal daily menu kicks in. Real ales include Bombardier, Ruddle's County, and Theakston's Old Peculier.

Telephone: *01773 810506*

The Walk

① Follow the road (**A608**) east from the **Sherwood Park** roundabout until you reach the entrance to **Home Farm**.

From Home Farm to the Annesley Hall entrance and back is no more than ¹/₂ mile, so you may wish to divert there before continuing. The hall was the home of the Chaworth-Musters family, one of the greater Nottinghamshire families. It is now in private hands, and not open to the public. The main entrance on the A608 is blocked off, but access to the ruined church – and a view of the old house – can be obtained via a short green lane beside that entrance.

Turn right at a bridleway guidepost close to the **Home Farm** entrance, and follow the metalled roadway. Keep to this track (**Weaver's Lane**) as it degrades to a gravel lane, ignoring a left turn. Cross the motorway bridge and pass **America Farm**. After passing through a short wooded section of path, the way emerges onto an open landscape before descending towards **Felley**. A glorious panorama opens up here of field and wood – while a convenient log invites you to pause and admire the view. (2 miles)

When I surveyed this route, within five minutes or so of putting the motorway behind me, I was able to take a welcome tea-break by the wayside, on another convenient log, in perfect peace, with just the breeze in the trees and the song of the birds for company – and a cheerful greeting from a passing stranger: 'How-do, my owd!' as he strolled on by with his terrier.

② Turn right at a junction of ways – the leftward track leads past the site of Felley Mill, immortalised in Lawrence's *The White Peacock*. Despite a diligent search, I failed to find it; so presumably it is no more. Follow the road – **Felley Mill Lane** – past **Felley Farm** and continue, to reach, and cross, the **A608**. Continue up **Sandhills Road**, crossing the **B600** and continuing along the enclosed footpath opposite. Cross an intervening road; go slightly left to follow the continuing path and then turn right along **Old Chapel Lane**. Continue ahead at the end, following the field path past a farm and stables, and then turn right at a guide post, descending over the fields to join the road at **Bagthorpe** and turning left. The **Shepherd's Rest** is a little way on, on the right. (2 miles)

THE SHEPHERD'S REST AT BAGTHORPE

Felley is one of Nottinghamshire's 'lost villages' – and little more today than a name on the map. As well as the mill (and the farm), there used to be a 12th century Augustinian priory here, but little of the monastic buildings now remains. The house that now occupies the site – on the A608, just north of Felley Mill Lane – is Elizabethan. The gardens, laid out where the priory church once stood, are open to the public. (Telephone: 01773 810230)

③ A footpath leaves the road just to the left of the **Shepherd's Rest**. The guidepost has two arms – the one to follow is the rightward one, which directs you over the fields to the rear of the pub.

Gaze around you and marvel as you cross these fields at the pure rural nature of the views, totally unblemished by industry, as far as the eye can see. It is difficult to conceive that all of this, even the actual fields on which you stand, was once a part of one of England's most productive coalfields.

Join **Inkerman Road** (the name, and that of neighbouring **Alma Road**, provides a guide to the age of the little estate) and, after following this for a little way, branch left onto an enclosed, descending footpath. Turn right at **Sperry Close**,

then left at **Nottingham Road** and cross over. Turn right by **Selston C of E School**, following the waymarked footpath along the track and over the fields to **Stoney Lane**. (1¹/₂ miles)

Another opportunity presents itself here for a brief extension. As at Annesley, the distance to Selston church and back is no more than ¹/₂ mile. The churchyard is the last resting place of Dan Boswell (1737–1827), the King of the Gypsies. The original gravestone is no longer legible, but a replacement bears the original inscription:

I've lodged in many a town, I've travelled many a year, But death at length has brought me down To my last lodging here.

The gypsies, it is said, still came here for many years after Dan's death, to pay their respects and to have their children baptised in the church.

④ Follow **Stoney Lane** east. Where the road bends right, take a footpath on the bend (left). Again, there is a choice of two paths here – take the rightward one, travelling in the same direction as before, with the hedge on your right. Turn right at **Commonside**; then left at a T-junction. Turn right again along **Portland Road** and left at **Bourne**

ON THE WALK NEAR INKERMAN

Avenue, leaving finally via a footpath on the right, immediately after the last house. The way from here is enclosed for the next $1/2$ mile and not heavily used. Cross **Salmon Lane**, bearing right a little to reach a waymarked farm track – and much easier, more pleasant walking. Immediately after crossing the **M1**, turn sharp right, leaving the farm track and taking a stepped footpath descending through the trees. Continue straight on as the path bears away from the

motorway, ignoring a side path on the left, and continue back to the **A608**. $(2^{1}/_{2}$ miles)

(Those seeking adventure will no doubt be overjoyed to learn that, at one point between Underwood and Bagthorpe, I was challenged by a very large and disagreeable Alsatian. He was securely chained and corralled, so was more disturbing than dangerous. But if you are worried, you can always retreat and find an alternative route. There is plenty of choice!)

Date walk completed:

NEWSTEAD PARK, BLIDWORTH AND FOUNTAIN DALE

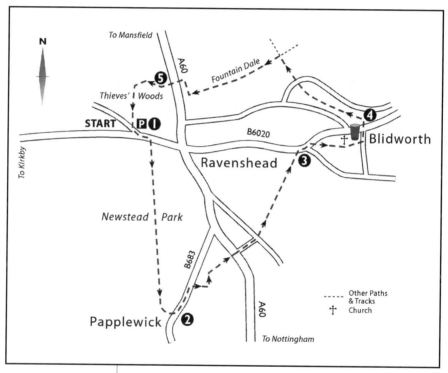

Distance:
11 miles

Starting point:
Thieves' Wood car park, Ravenshead. (Grid reference: SK 541558)

Maps: OS Landranger 120 (Mansfield and Worksop)
OS Explorer 270 (Sherwood Forest)

How to get there: *From the A60 (Larch Farm crossroads) turn west onto the B6020 (Kirkby in Ashfield road). Turn right again at the B6139. Thieves' Wood car park is on the right.*

THE TRACK LEADING TO PROVIDENCE FARM, BLIDWORTH

*M*ost of this walk, in keeping with the popular traditions of Sherwood Forest, follows sections of the Robin Hood Way, a tortuous route around much of Sherwood and beyond devised by my old friends of the Nottingham Wayfarers Rambling Club. I make no apologies for this. The guys and gals of the Wayfs always were dab hands at identifying a good path, track or green lane.

History, romance and legend meet in this fascinating corner of Sherwood Forest. Thieves' Wood, where we start, is typical of the old forest – a patchwork of woodland and heath – and the name is interesting. Could it be a reference to Robin Hood and his band? The poet Lord Byron – mad, bad and dangerous to know, according to Lady Caroline Lamb – lived at Newstead Abbey, through the wooded parkland of which we pass in the earliest stages of our walk. We continue by forest and field paths to Blidworth, the traditional home of Maid Marian and the last resting place of Will Scarlet, and it is here that we pause for a well-earned bite and a tipple. Then on to Fountain Dale, where, we are told, Robin Hood received his come-uppance from Friar Tuck.

The Bird in Hand, on Blidworth's Main Street, is a pub with a view. Not particularly eye-catching from the road, it is most attractive from the rear – and it is from here, in the dining area and the beautifully laid out beer garden, that that glorious panorama of field and forest can best be appreciated. This is a Wolverhampton and Dudley house, with, so we are told, its own resident ghost. Visitors will find a ready welcome and friendly service here, supported by a wide range of nourishing home-made meals and traditional Mansfield ales. Food is served daily from Monday to Saturday, between 12 noon and 2 pm and from 6 pm to 8 pm, when all tastes are catered for from a menu which includes grills and steaks, and hot and cold snacks. Additional options, as well as a vegetarian selection, are displayed on the specials board, and there is a separate menu for the children. The only food served on Sundays is a traditional Sunday roast with all the trimmings (and a choice of large, medium or small helpings), which is available from 12 noon until 3 pm, and for which prior booking is advisable.

Telephone: *01623 401221*

① Turn left out of the car park, following the road to its junction with the B6020 and turning left again. Cross the road and continue past **High Leys Drive** until you reach a waymarked footpath on the right. Follow this enclosed path, passing to the left of an estate of large modern houses and continuing then on the left of the field, with a greystone wall on your left. After entering the **Newstead Abbey** estate, follow a delightful wooded path that descends to cross the metalled access road through **Swinecotte Dale**.

This Swinecotte Dale road leads down to Newstead Abbey, the home of the poet Lord Byron, and a popular tourist attraction. Not visible from the footpath, the abbey and grounds are well worth a visit – and there is no logical reason, of course, why you should not incorporate such a visit into your ramble. It has to be mentioned though, that, although there is a public right of way along the footpath, this does not extend to the rest of the abbey grounds, which are in the custody of the City of Nottingham and subject to a possible entrance fee away from the path.

Keeping on along the wooded path, you emerge eventually onto

59

another metalled road. Follow this on to a pair of lodge gates, diverting right to bypass the driveway, before rejoining the road, now reverted to the status of a green lane. Approaching **Papplewick**, bear left with the track to join **Blidworth Waye** (the **B683**) and turn left. (2 miles)

② Cross the road and follow the ascending, stepped footpath – a highly satisfactory alternative to the hard road. This eventually descends to continue through the roadside trees. Turn right opposite the entrance to **Newstead Grange**, and follow the hedge and a row of pylons up a very long field. Turn left on reaching a wood, following the woodside path to a guidepost, where the path bends right, through the trees. Continue over woodland and heath, crossing a rough track and keeping to the waymarked path to reach the main (**A60**) road. Cross over and follow **Kighill Lane** to its junction with **Longdale Lane**. Ignore the private drive immediately opposite, bearing left to join the parallel field path on the corner of **Chapel Lane**. Keep straight ahead now, following the field boundary for about 1½ miles to arrive at the **B6020**. (3 miles)

③ Keep straight on ahead along the road, passing the minor road on your right, and continuing to a footpath stile, also on the right.

Follow the field path over a series of arable fields for about a mile to **Field Lane**, just outside **Blidworth**. Turn left and ascend the hill into the village, following Main Street round to the left to reach the **Bird in Hand**. (1½ miles)

The hilltop village of Blidworth has played host to a variety of rogues, vagabonds and outlaws over the centuries, some of them baddies, but most of them – in popular tradition at least – goodies. Forest Folk, James Prior's story of the Industrial Revolution, tells of the struggles between the framework knitters of the town and the Luddite machine breakers. But the village is perhaps better known as the last resting place of Will Scarlet, one of Robin Hood's right-hand men, and the home, before her marriage to Robin, of Maid Marian. And it was in this neighbourhood, as we shall find later, that Friar Tuck was recruited into the happy band of Merry Men.

Industrial discord and popular legend aside, St Mary's church in Blidworth is the venue, on the first Sunday in February each year, of a 'Rocking Ceremony', when the male child born in the parish closest to Christmas is ceremoniously rocked in a flower-decked cradle.

④ Leaving the **Bird in Hand**, turn

THIEVES' WOOD AT THE BEGINNING OF THE WALK

right and cross the road, looking for a footpath on your left. This climbs steeply between walls to reach the fields, continuing ahead along the field boundary and descending over a series of fields to emerge onto a farm track. Turn left here and continue beside the wood and along the succeeding enclosed path. On reaching **New Lane**, cross the road and follow the farm track to **Providence Farm**. Pass to the left of the farm and through a bridle-gate to reach, and cross, **Fountain Dale**.

It was here, according to popular tradition, that Robin Hood first made the acquaintance of the Fat Friar – and received a drenching for his trouble. Rainworth Water and its ponds were evidently in far better condition in those days. The dale is overgrown and neglected today, and anyone wishing to follow Robin's example will need to be very determined. But if all else fails, a mud bath is not impossible – especially if you try to locate Friar Tuck's Well,

which is also marked on the map, but for which I have sought in vain.

Turn left, following the dale. The path, initially rather meandering and uncertain, widens and improves after a while. Ignore any turnings and deviations, keeping straight ahead through the forest until, just short of the **A60** road, the track turns right, continuing parallel to the road. On reaching the **Portland Training College** buildings, turn left and continue to the road. (3^1/$_4$ miles)

⑤ Cross the road with care – it can be very busy – and carry on ahead, following a school boundary fence. Bear right with the track, continuing to a T-junction and turning left. Branch left in the dip and continue back to the **Thieves' Wood** car park. (1^1/$_4$ miles)

Date walk completed:

SOUTHWELL TO OXTON, AND ROBIN HOOD HILL

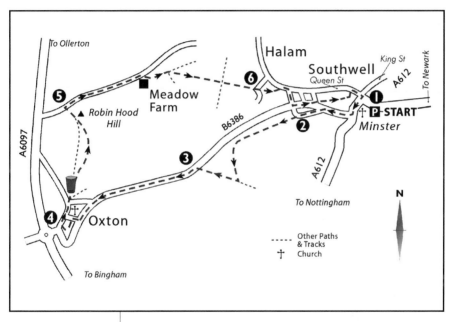

Distance:
12¹/₂ miles.

Starting point:
Southwell, Church Street public car park.
(Grid reference: SK 701539)

Maps: OS Landranger 120 (Mansfield and Worksop)
OS Explorer 28 (270) (Sherwood Forest)

How to get there: *The cathedral village of Southwell stands on the A612 (Nottingham to Newark road) and can also be reached from Mansfield via the A617, turning right at Hockerton.*

LOOKING WEST FROM ROBIN HOOD HILL

*W*e come about as near to hill-walking as we possibly can on this walk – though I suspect the Peak District purists might scoff at the comparison. But who cares? Robin Hood Hill tops out at around 500 feet, with views, so 'tis said, of four counties. After leaving Southwell car park, we follow the road west to the adjacent village of Westhorpe before traversing the fields – both grass and arable – for a couple of miles. An unavoidable road walk from here brings us to Oxton, and our welcome lunch break.

Having satisfied the inner person, we come to our delightful little hill climb – not at all strenuous, and doubly welcome after that road walk – which brings us to the site of the Iron Age settlement of Oldox, and to Robin Hood Hill with its glorious views. Our return journey follows the Robin Hood Way for much of the distance, along a quiet country lane and over pleasant hill tracks, to the outskirts of Southwell, from where it is a short and satisfying stroll back to the town – and its many features of interest.

Ye Olde Bridge Inn, in Nottingham Road, Oxton, is smart and modern (in the nicest possible way!) with welcoming staff and a busy, cheerful atmosphere. Opening time is all day every day, and food is served from Tuesday to Saturday between 12 noon and 9 pm and from 12 noon until 5 pm on Sundays. Steaks and grills are a speciality of the house, and other favourites include steak and ale pie, hickory chicken, seafood platter and vegetable lasagne. There is a tasty selection of baguettes, jacket potatoes and salads and the whole menu is supplemented by the ubiquitous 'writing on the wall' – the bar blackboard. A traditional roast is served on Sundays. Real ales include Theakston's.

Telephone: *0115 965 2013*
Alternative refreshment facilities can be found at the **Green Dragon**, *in Blind Lane, Oxton: open all day Saturday and Sunday from 12 noon, and evenings only, from 5 pm, in the week. There is no set menu, but food can be provided to order – and we understand that the management is prepared to make special arrangements for walking groups if advised the previous day (telephone 0115 965 2012).* **The Minster Refectory**, *in Church Street, Southwell, is specially recommended for light meals and snacks either before or after your walk (telephone 01636 815691).*

① Leaving the car park, turn right along **Church Street**, then left by the **Saracen's Head**. Pass the Nottingham turning and continue ahead along the **B6386**. Branch left after passing the **Dumbles** pub, following the unclassified road through **Westhorpe** village. (1¼ miles)

There is a uniqueness about Southwell, where this walk begins and ends, for it is a village – not a city – that is able to boast its own cathedral. It is also famous as the home of the Bramley apple. The village's name, incidentally, is contentious. The natives, I understand, pronounce it as written: South-well. The 'off-comers', and the racing fraternity, call it Suthall.

② Where the metalled lane bends right, keep straight forward, following a tree-lined lane. When this fades out, continue ahead, now following the left-hand side of the hedge over the fields. Turn right through a gateway; then go left over a stile. Cross the end of the field and turn right, following the hedge.

Turn left again at the top end of the field and follow the farm track down the centre of this long one, to cross a green lane, continuing over a stile and on. In the next field, follow the hedge right and left to reach a stile, giving access to a country lane.

A sign beside the stile at this point informs us that the land we have just left belongs to Thorney Abbey Farm, 'home of the Lottabottle herd of pedigree Holstein cattle', which is managed with the welfare of both the stock and the environment in mind. The various avian varieties identified in the area have included skylarks and lapwings, sparrowhawks, tawny owls and a breeding pair of buzzards; while wildflowers seen in season along the field margins and hedgerows include cowslips and violets. 'Enjoy your walk!' says the sign – which is nice.

Turn right along the lane and continue to the **Southwell/Oxton** road (**B6386**). (2 miles)

③ Turn left. Although a busy road, there is a wide grass verge for most of the way to **Oxton**. The exception to this is on **Oxton Hill**, where the road seems to narrow and one or two blind bends occur. Extreme care is advised on this stretch, keeping in file, well in to the edge on the right-hand side of the road. Pass **Blind Lane** and take the next turning on the right (**Sandy Lane**). Turn left immediately after the ford, following **Water Lane** through to **Main Street**. **Ye Olde Bridge** is directly opposite. (2½ miles)

YE OLDE BRIDGE INN, OXTON

④ Follow **Main Street** through the village, passing the church. Turn right at **Blind Lane**, then immediately left by the **Green Dragon**, following **Windmill Hill** gently uphill and enjoying the opening views over to your left as you ascend. Just after passing a bench the way branches. Both routes provide access to **Robin Hood Hill** and **Oldox Camp**, and there is little if any difference in the distance. Having said that (and having tried them both) I can recommend the rightward track – a permissive path – as the better. After a shortish initial length of green lane, this follows the field side, bending left and right at one point to cross a stile and reach the Iron Age site, passing along its left-hand edge.

The Iron Age hill-fort of Oldox, and the adjacent Bronze Age barrow are believed to be the only prehistoric sites of any importance in Nottinghamshire. The fort is small, measuring only 1¹/₂ acres in area, with a bank, ditch and counterscarp bank on the west side and three banks and ditches on the east. There was an entrance on the north-west side and, possibly, another on the south-east (Observer's Book of Ancient and Roman Britain –Harold Priestley/Frederick Warne and Co Ltd, 1976).

Turn right with the fence at the north-western corner of the site to reach and cross a stile. Turn left then to follow the main path along the left side of a fence, before curving around to the right of **Robin Hood Hill** to reach its summit, a super place for a rest, and a picnic if you are so inclined (but take your rubbish home afterwards). Kinder Scout it ain't, but the views all around, and especially to the west, over farm, field and forest, are magnificent. Descend carefully north-west to regain the main path at a stile, continuing beside **Loath Hill Wood** and bearing left over the field at the end to join a track leading down to **Greaves Lane**. (2 miles)

⑤ Follow **Greaves Lane** east for about a mile, passing **Hartswell Farm** and **Wood Farm** – respectively on the left and the right. Turn right immediately after **Meadow Farm**, following the farm track as directed by a **Robin Hood Way** sign at the entrance. Keep to the left of a farm gate and continue along a woodland path to reach a seat and a stone structure bearing a tablet which indicates that this is the mid-way point (and one of the highest spots) on the **Robin Hood Way**.

The Robin Hood Way was created by the Nottingham Wayfarers' Rambling Club in 1982, to commemorate their golden jubilee, the object of the exercise being to devise a route that would visit all the sites in the county associated with our favourite baddie/goodie. It probably does, but those sites are so many and so widely distributed that, in order to fit them all in, the architects of the route have had to provide spurs branching off in all directions. Meadow Farm being on one of those spurs, I must confess to some little uncertainty as to how the location of the seat and tablet has been identified as the half-way point!

The seat is well placed for a sneaky break, and to admire the view over **Farnsfield**, before joining the nearby minor road. Keep straight ahead here, but turn right on reaching a green lane on the right, swinging left with the track by **Little Turncroft Farm**. After crossing another minor road, the way continues as a field path, following a low ridge, and providing wide views in every direction. A delightfully wooded section follows as we descend to pass **Machin's Farm**. Turn left over a stile and cross

a footbridge to reach the **Manor Fields Estate**, then follow the access road to **Halam** (pronounced Hay-lam) village street and turn right. (2³/₄ miles)

⑥ Turn left and right with the road to reach a footpath leading off left. Follow the wooded way to a stile, which you cross, and continue along the hedge-side on your left. As the hedge bends left, continue straight ahead over the field, passing to the right of a hollow, to reach another stile. Keep straight ahead now, following the field boundaries past a nursery, to reach the road and turn right. Turn left on reaching the **B6380**. Ignore the first turning (**Cooke Lane**) and continue to a cottage, where a footpath leads off left. Follow the field path beside the hedge, crossing a residential road and continuing along the same line past a couple of housing estates and a school playing field. Turn left with the fenced path and continue to the road (**Queen Street**). Turn right again at **King Street** and left by the **Saracen's Head** to reach the car park. (2 miles)

 *Date walk completed:*

KIRKLINGTON TO HOCKERTON AND THE SOUTHWELL TRAIL

THE HALL ENTRANCE, WINKBURN

Distance:
10½ miles
Starting point:
Kirklington station.
(Grid reference:
SK 676566)

Maps: OS Landranger 120 (Mansfield and Worksop)
OS Explorer 28 (270) (Sherwood Forest) and 271
(Newark-on-Trent)

How to get there: Kirklington village is on the A617 (Mansfield to Newark road), about 3½ miles east of the A614. Turn south at the western end of the village, following Southwell Road. Then take the first turning on the right, branching right again along the narrow 'Southwell Trail' access road.

*T*here are parts of Nottinghamshire where it is possible to walk all day and never meet a living soul – and this is one of them. The walk begins at Kirklington station on the Southwell Trail – a former branch of the Midland Railway closed to traffic many years ago and now enjoying a new lease of life as a popular recreational route. Bypassing Kirklington village, we set off across open country to Roe Wood, and the highest ground of the day, from where the distant views are among the most impressive. Close by is the village of Maplebeck, a haven of peace, which boasts – just off our route, as it happens – the tiniest pub in Nottinghamshire. A quiet road is followed from here to pretty little Winkburn, so small that if you do wink you have a fair chance of missing it, whence we take the field path route to Hockerton and our lunch stop. The byways followed on the second half of our journey are, theoretically, rather more populous – but you are likely to find that fellow walkers, even here, are something of a rarity. Continuing from Hockerton to the outskirts of Southwell, we rejoin the trail for the final stage of a delightful and rewarding walk.

The **Spread Eagle**, in Caunton Road, Hockerton, has proprietors who are themselves keen walkers and you are assured of a warm welcome. This former forge is an Inn-spired plc house with a beautiful open fireplace in the beamed bar-room, brass- and copper-ware on the hearth, and a bijou bar counter. There is a tiled patio at the rear, where visiting walkers are asked to park their boots, if muddy, before entering the pub. Families are welcome and there is an outside drinking area as well as a non-smoking zone. Opening hours are from 12 noon until 2.30 pm and 6.30 pm till 11 pm Tuesday to Saturday; from 12 noon until 3 pm and 7 pm until 10.30 pm on Sundays. Monday is the proprietors' day off.

Food is served between 12 noon and 2 pm every day (except Monday, of course) and in the evening from 6.30 pm till 8.30 pm Tuesday to Friday (6.30 pm until 9 pm on Saturday). The menu is impressive, specialities of the house including steak, mushroom and ale pie, haddock supreme, and Hockerton honey roast ham with egg and chips. Vegetarians are also catered for and there is a choice of delicious sandwiches and salads for those of simpler taste. The traditional Sunday lunch includes a selection of starters,

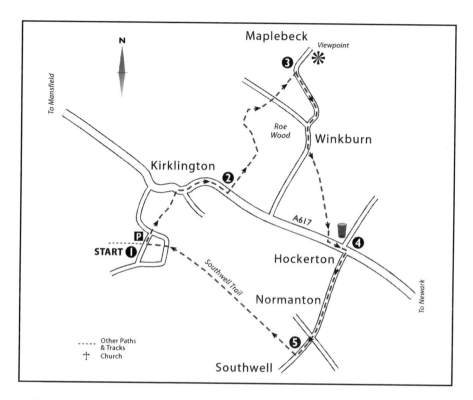

main courses and sweets. Real ales include Mansfield Cask Bitter and two guest beers.

Telephone: *01636 812019*

 **The Walk**

① Leaving the station area, turn left along the road and then right at the next junction. Go left again at a guidepost, following the route of the **Robin Hood Way** along the field's edge. Bear left over a footbridge

and turn right, still following the field's edge and, after passing a large pond, recross the brook. The path branches now, so take the rightward option, crossing straight ahead over the field to reach and cross a stile beside a farm gate. Continue left, crossing a farm track and passing through a wood. Emerging on the far side of the wood, turn right along its edge and continue to the road, passing a farm and turning right onto the **A617**. Ignore a side turning (**Corkhill Lane**) on your right and continue up the hill. (1¹/₄ miles)

② Leave the road on the brow of the hill, using the squeezer to the left of a farm gate and turning right immediately to follow the farm track over a broad open plain. Where the track bends right, keep straight ahead along a lesser, green hedge-side way. Keep straight on at another junction of tracks, now following the edge of the ditch. Curve left with the path, ignoring a

single ditch-board on the right, and, where the path bends again, right and then left, cross two successive double plank bridges and follow the edge of **Roe Wood**. Keep to the perimeter around two sides of the wood; then turn left to pass through a gateway, crossing the succeeding field on a direct line to arrive at a minor lane. The path continues on the opposite side of the road, crossing it on a diagonal line as directed by the guidepost. Cross a footbridge in the dip (somewhere around here, according to the map, there is a holy well – but I failed to spot it). Cross this bigger field on a straight line, making for the highest

THE SPREAD EAGLE INN, HOCKERTON, WAS ONCE A FORGE

ground, just to the left of a distant pylon, to emerge on a bend of the **Maplebeck** road. (2¹/₄ miles)

A little way on along the road is the Maplebeck viewpoint, incorporating a parking and picnic area. There are no significant peaks around here, only relatively gentle gradients culminating in this single highest point, but the altitude and the views alone are sufficient to justify the presence of a viewfinder detailing the distances to a number of locations around this and neighbouring counties. It should be possible to make out Lincoln Cathedral; Nottingham Castle, on the other hand, is unlikely.

Although Maplebeck village is not on the official itinerary, energetic connoisseurs of good pubs might consider it worth their while to add on an extra mile by skipping down to the village and back to enjoy the hospitality of the Beehive – a marvellous little pub which boasts the distinction of being the smallest in Nottinghamshire.

③ From the viewpoint, follow the road back round the bend and continue to **Winkburn**, a tiny but attractive village.

Winkburn is 'on the Wink' – that being the name of the stream which runs through the village. Or

so the OS map says. My (pre-war) copy of Arthur Mee's Nottinghamshire calls it the River Wink, which sounds a little pretentious to me – as does Cornelius Brown's 'River Winkle' in his 1896 History of Nottinghamshire. Then again, the name of the village suggests that it is the Wink Burn, but we do not have many burns in the East Midlands! Perhaps we had better stick with the Ordnance Survey title. From the 12th century until the reign of Henry VIII, Winkburn belonged to the Knights Hospitallers of St John of Jerusalem.

Follow the road through the village, crossing a grassy triangle by the hall entrance and negotiating a stile onto the fields. Bear right a little as you cross the field, through a depression, to reach a second stile in the angle of the fence. Keep on ahead, making for the right-hand corner of a triangular strip of woodland. Cross the next field, again on a diagonal line, turning left through the gap then to follow the hedge for a short distance. Turn right, again following the right of the hedge, and continuing, as directed by the yellow arrows, to reach the road (**A617**). Turn left for **Hockerton** and the **Spread Eagle**. (3 miles)

The Hockerton Housing Project is

a unique little development of five earth sheltered, self-sufficient ecological homes, which has won national acclaim with the bestowal of environmental and energy saving awards. The residents live a holistic way of life in harmony with the environment, generating their own energy, harvesting their own water and recycling all their waste.

④ Leaving the pub, continue on along the **A617**, taking the first turning on the right. Follow this through to the outskirts of **Southwell**, crossing the **River Greet** and passing the **Greet Mill** before turning right onto the **Southwell Trail** car park. (1¹/₂ miles)

The Southwell Trail follows the route of the former Southwell to Farnsfield railway line, itself a

section of the Mansfield to Southwell branch of the Midland Railway, which opened in 1871. Farnsfield and Kirklington stations were both closed to passenger traffic in 1929, but the line remained open to goods traffic until 1964, after which the route was designated as a recreational path.

⑤ Follow the trail back to **Kirklington station**. The way is very peaceful and rural, especially as **Southwell** is left behind and the track becomes shrouded in trees and bordered by open fields. The occasional benches provided along the way are particularly welcome. (2¹/₂ miles)

Date walk completed:

74

PULPIT ASH, RUFFORD PARK AND WELLOW MAYPOLE

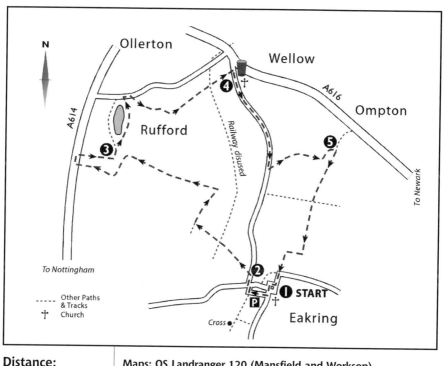

Distance: 11¼ miles

Starting point: Kirklington Road, Eakring. (Grid reference: SK 675622)

Maps: OS Landranger 120 (Mansfield and Worksop)
OS Explorer 28 (270) (Sherwood Forest)

How to get there: *Follow the A614 north from Nottingham, continuing beyond the A617 roundabout for 2½ miles and turning right for Eakring. Kirklington Road is towards the end of the village, on the right, and the best place to park is on the roadside by the church.*

*F*rom Eakring, we follow the Robin Hood Way over a wide and open landscape to Rufford Country Park, where we pause to enjoy the beautiful lake and other facilities. From here we continue to Wellow, a conservation village, and one of Nottinghamshire's prettiest, where the ancient tradition of dancing round the maypole on May Day still survives.

The Olde Red Lion, in Eakring Road, Wellow, dates back to the 17th century. Although converted to its present use only in the 1920s – previously it was a row of cottages – the house has all the atmosphere of a traditional country pub. There is a tiny little entrance lobby-cum-taproom known as 'The Nook' and two larger rooms where diners and drinkers may stretch out their legs while satisfying their appetites. The outside is equally attractive, with tables overlooking the village green and the maypole. Food is served daily, from 11.30 am to 2.30 pm in the week and from 12 noon until 3.30 pm on Saturdays and Sundays. Evening meals are available every day (including Sunday) from 6 pm until 10 pm. Prices are reasonable and the menu covers all tastes: chicken dishes, fish and grills, sandwiches and specials. Vegetarians and children are specially catered for, and the range of 'Red Lion Favourites' includes – not surprisingly – Maypole Delight, consisting of delicious ham served with salad and harvest grain bread. Families are welcome; so too are well-behaved dogs, but only outside please – unless, of course, they are guide dogs.

Telephone: *01623 861000*
Alternative refreshment facilities: the **Coach House Coffee Shop***, in Rufford Park (telephone: 01623 822944); the* **Savile Arms,** *in Main Street, Eakring – drink only, no food (telephone: 01623 870264).*

 *The Walk*

Eakring can claim a place in history as the birthplace of the British oil industry. You will find

no mighty gushers here, nor is there any possibility of our wells putting Texas and Iraq out of business. Our modest contribution has been confined to those sturdy but agreeable beasts, the nodding donkeys. The first successful wells

THE MAYPOLE AT WELLOW GREEN IS SAID TO BE THE TALLEST IN THE COUNTRY

were sunk in 1939 and made a valuable contribution to the national economy during the 1939-45 war.

① Follow **Church Lane** (opposite the village church), turning left when you reach a T-junction to follow the farm lane as it bends right and left. **Mompesson's Cross** is about ¼ mile on, just off the lane to its right.

William Mompesson came to Eakring round about 1670, four years or so after his harrowing experiences at Eyam, where the bubonic plague – brought from London in a bundle of clothes – had carried off at least 70% of his flock, including his wife. When he first arrived here, the villagers

refused to allow him into the church – or the village – and for some time he was exiled to a hut in Rufford Park. His little cross stands on a low rise in a fenced enclosure, at the spot known as Pulpit Ash, where, throughout his exile, Mompesson preached to those of his parishioners who remained loyal. The story has a happier ending, for William was eventually accepted by the parish and remained here until his death in 1708.

Leaving the cross, we return to **Church Lane**, continuing straight forward to reach **Main Street**. Turn left here, then right again by the **Savile Arms**, following **Wellow Road** until you reach a stile on the

77

left, beside a metal farm gate. (1 mile)

② Over the stile, cross the field on a direct line, bearing half-right over a second stile, to continue over two more vast fields. The path does not appear to be heavily used but is easy to follow, keeping to the highest ground and providing wide views in every direction. After crossing another stile, the path descends to cross a defunct railway cutting, continuing via a footbridge and heading for **Rufford Park**. Turn right on reaching a broad farm track, crossing **Gallow Hole Dyke**

and turning left by **North Laiths Farm**. Where the track forks, keep left, following the concrete roadway past a block of stables etc. The track emerges via a pedestrian gate to continue over a golf course. Turn left with the track and cross a bridge over **Rainworth Water**, branching left again at the next junction. (A 'Private' notice on this junction can be ignored, as can a similar one where the route meets the **A614**. Both of these can be taken as referring purely to vehicular traffic, the Nottinghamshire County Council Rights of Way Department having confirmed that this section of the

THE OLDE RED LION IN WELLOW

route is a public right of way on foot.) Turn right again after passing a small bungalow, following a gravelled track lined with poplar trees. Keep to the left of the buildings as you pass **Manor Farm**, continuing on to join the **A614**. Turn right and follow the **A614** for $^1/_4$ mile, turning right then as for the **Rufford Abbey** car park. Follow the access road through to the Stable Block, a good place to pause for refreshments (at the **Coach House Coffee Shop**), or for toilets, etc. ($3^1/_2$ miles)

Rufford Abbey was founded by Gilbert de Gant in 1146 as a daughter house of Rievaulx Abbey. Having 'inherited' the property following the dissolution of the monasteries, the sixth Earl of Shrewsbury converted it into a country house. The estate later passed into the hands of the Saviles, who retained it until 1938. The army took over during the Second World War, after which it fell into disrepair. The whole property, including the country park, is now in the care of Nottinghamshire County Council.

③ Follow the access paths to the **lake**, where you may choose to follow either the left bank or the right. The right is the longer, and the more delightful, but either route will bring you to the **Wellow Road** car park. Turn right along the road,

passing the water-splash (and taking care to avoid being drenched by over-enthusiastic motorists). At the golf club entrance, cross a stile on the left to join and follow the adjacent farm road. The path skirts round to the right of **Rufford Hills Farm**, following the hedge round to cross a stile and rejoin the farm road. Turn right here, bearing right again where the road bends, to follow a field track. Reaching a dog-leg bend in the track, turn left to follow a path over the field, making for a distant solitary tree; on reaching it, bear a little to the right and continue over this field and the next. The route now crosses the same derelict railway line crossed earlier. The cutting is very deep – 73 steps down and 69 up, according to my reckoning, all of them in poor condition. Be aware that horse-riders use the grass tracks in the bed of the cutting for a gallop. If you prefer, you can retreat and join the **Wellow** road – but you are reminded that the only accessible route is not currently dedicated as a right of way. Having crossed the cutting, the rest is all plain sailing. Cross a stile, continuing along the field-side to reach the road and turn left for **Wellow** village green – and the **Olde Red Lion**. ($2^1/_2$ miles)

A pretty and peaceful conservation village today, Wellow was not always so. In former times it was fortified with a dyke and earthworks to protect the people and livestock from pillaging neighbours. And the relationship with the abbot and monks of Rufford was always difficult, from its foundation in the 12th century until the dissolution. Many of the properties still enjoy grazing rights – or tofts – on the common greens. But the most prominent feature of the village today is the permanent maypole, said to be the tallest in the country. Erected in 1976 to replace the former timber pole, the present one is made of steel, and still provides a focus each year for the traditional May Day festivities.

④ Follow **Eakring Road** south, keeping well in to the right-hand side after the pavement ends and watching for approaching traffic. After passing a pumping station (with attractive modern buildings), turn sharp left – 100+ degrees – by the **Little Leyfield** driveway entrance and follow the waymarked bridleway over the field. The path bends right a little at the rear of the pumping station, passing to the left of an electricity pylon to meet and cross a minor farm track, after which it continues as a pleasant green lane. After swinging left, the lane reverts to a farm track. (2$^1/_4$ miles)

⑤ As the village of **Ompton** comes into view ahead, turn right over a footbridge and follow the footpath over the fields. The route keeps to a relatively straight line, in sync if not in close touch with the neighbouring hedges, over the first three fields, before crossing a stile in the field corner and continuing to **Leyfields Farm**. Pass to the right of the farm buildings and continue via the gravelled farm road. After crossing four cattle grids, bear right over one field and pass through the gap, turning left then to follow the field-side track. Turn right at the road, following it round to reach **Eakring** village, and then left into **Kirklington Road**. (2 miles)

Date walk completed:

FAITH AND TRADITION AROUND LAXTON'S FIELDS

THE VILLAGE OF LAXTON IS WELL WORTH EXPLORING

Distance:
10 miles

Starting point:
Visitor Centre car park, Dovecote Inn, Laxton.
(Grid reference: SK 724671)

Maps: OS Landranger 120 (Mansfield and Worksop)
OS Explorer 271 (Newark-on-Trent)

How to get there: *From the Ollerton roundabout, follow the A6076 through New Ollerton and Boughton. Where the main road bends sharp left, take the unclassified road straight ahead, passing under the railway bridge and continuing for about 2¹/₂ miles to Laxton. The Dovecote Inn and Visitor Centre are on the road junction at the eastern end of the village. (Please ensure that you use the visitor centre car park, not the pub's parking spaces.)*

*T*his walk offers a wealth of interest, most of it with either a religious or a traditional connotation – for which we make no apologies, religion and tradition both being endemic to our national makeup. The walk centres round the village of Laxton, where the medieval three-field system of agriculture still survives. Leaving Laxton, we journey first to the neighbouring village of Egmanton, where a claimed vision of the Blessed Virgin is still remembered. From here we skirt around the perimeter of Laxton's West Field to reach the Holocaust memorial centre at Beth Shalom – where the memories are more disturbing, and much more recent. Continuing our circular tour we reach Kneesall village; here an angel is a synonym for good food and drink! And so we continue, over the Mill Field, back to Laxton. This is a longish walk – but some time set aside either before or after the walk to explore the various points of interest in Laxton village itself – including the visitor centre and the site of a motte and bailey – will not be wasted.

The Angel Inn – a free house in Main Street, Kneesall – was built about 300 years ago, and stands at the eastern end of this village. It has a somewhat modest and reclusive – though not unattractive – outward appearance, which, combined with its situation, might easily cause it to be passed unawares. Which would be unfortunate to say the least! The half-timbered interior is full of character and there is a ready welcome for all, with a family room, children's play area, smoke-free zone and beer garden. The opening hours are from 11.30 am (11.45 on Sundays) until 3 pm, and in the evenings from 6 pm until 11 pm.

If you are looking for a full meal, the choice of starters alone is impressive. The speciality of the house is its range of individually grilled steaks, which include fillet Stilton, Angel peppered steak, and 'Lump' of lamb. Fish dishes are another speciality, and there is a wide selection of vegetarian and children's meals, rolls, salads, ploughman's selections and extra portions. There is always a good range of real ales, and all the food is home cooked.

Telephone: *01623 861078*
*Alternative refreshment facilities will be found at the **Old Plough**, Main Street, Egmanton (telephone: 01777 872565); or at the **Dovecote** in Laxton (telephone: 01777 871586).*

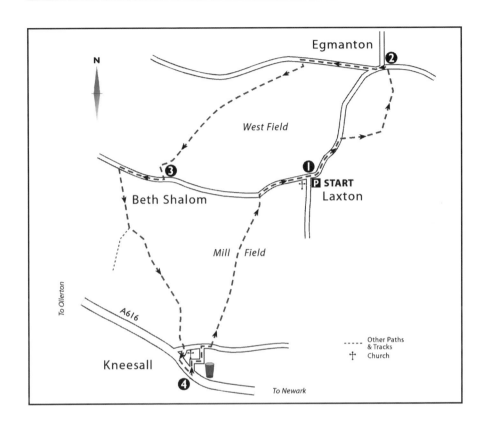

 *The Walk*

① Turn right out of the car park, leaving the village via **Egmanton Road**.

Laxton is the last place in the country to retain the ancient 'open field' system of agriculture, still unchanged in its essentials from the pattern established throughout the land 1,000 years

or more ago. Four hundred and eighty three acres are still farmed under the old system, consisting of three fields: Mill Field, South Field and West Field; two of these are cropped in rotation each year while the third remains fallow. The management and operation of the open fields is administered by the Field Jury, which itself is responsible to the Court Leet. This meets in the Dovecote Inn in December to ensure that the requirements of the system are properly carried out, and to impose fines on those failing to do so.

Stay with the road, ignoring a waymarked track that leads off on the first (left-hand) bend, and continuing until you reach a bridleway on the right, just before **Egmanton Hill Farm**. There is a guidepost directly opposite. Turn right here, following the field-side. If the day is clear, you should be able to see, about 10 miles away to the north-east, the cooling towers of one of our county's power stations (West Drayton, if I am not mistaken). Keep to the track as it bends left and right, continuing past **Egmanton Wood** and on to **Egmanton** village. On reaching a T-junction, cross the field in front to reach the village church, and turn left. (2 miles)

The parish church in Egmanton is dedicated to Our Lady of Egmanton – unusual, perhaps, for an Anglican church. The devotion does not appear to be recognised by the Roman Catholic Church, but that need not necessarily invalidate it. The tradition began very many years ago when a local woman claimed to have seen a vision of the Blessed Virgin in what is now known as Ladywood, on the edge of the parish. The shrine was a prominent feature until its destruction in 1547, and an object of devout pilgrimage,

but following the reformation, and with the passing of time, the devotion became little more than a dim local memory. Until 1897, that is, when a detailed restoration of the building was carried out, which included the provision of a replacement image of the Virgin. Since that time, the old devotion has been revived, and the popularity of the shrine as a place of pilgrimage has steadily increased.

② Follow the road round, bearing right by the **Old Plough**, to follow an unclassified road. After passing an ultra-modern building (the map calls it **Bankside Farm**, but there was no evidence of agricultural activity when I passed), ignore the first lane on the left. Continue on, to take the next turning on the left (there is no waymark here). Reaching a gateway, pass through and turn right, following the hedge. The path here appears to be little used but should not present any difficulties. The hedge – and an accompanying ditch or stream – is followed for most of the way; the stiles are excellent, and the waymarks are adequate. Ignore a crossing path, which emerges from the wood on the right, and also a farm track which swings left across the field. Keep straight on, with the field boundary on your right, enjoying a pleasant mixture of grassland and arable. After passing through a gateway, continue ahead until you reach a left turn. Take this, and continue to the road, opposite the **Beth Shalom Holocaust Centre** – identified on the map as **Westwood Farm**. (3 miles)

Beth Shalom – or House of Peace – was established by two brothers, Stephen and James Smith, as a direct result of a family visit to the Holy Land in 1981. In the course of this visit they came to realise that the Holocaust was not simply a Jewish problem, but one that Gentiles as well should acknowledge and confront. Opened in 1995, the centre is set in two acres of gardens, and includes a range of facilities designed to assist people of all backgrounds and persuasions in exploring and understanding the implications of the Holocaust. The centre is open each week, Wednesday to Sunday, between 10 am and 5 pm, from January to November.

③ Follow the road west (right) for about ¼ mile over **Laxton Common**. Turn left opposite an access road and follow the bridleway to reach the eastern tip of **Wellow Park** woods at **Cocking Moor**. Cross the corner of the wood, turning left a little on emerging, to continue beside the hedge (left-hand

THE ATTRACTIVE ANGEL INN AT KNEESALL

side). Turn left at the far end of the field; then right to follow the track over two more fields. Continue right and left with the path to join the farm road at the south-east entrance to **Wood Close Farm**. Continue down the lane to **Kneesall**, crossing the unclassified road and continuing ahead to join **Main Street** (the **A616**) and turn left. The **Angel Inn** is on the left, just past the church. (2¹/₂ miles)

Historical information about Kneesall – a tidy little village on the Newark to Ollerton road, with a mixture of traditional and modern housing – is, regrettably, in short supply. White's Directory of 1853 describes it as a 'considerable village on a gentle declivity'. Rather more fascinating is the news that a wood called

'Hertshorne' was once held on lease by Richard Markham and William Sutton for an annual payment of two shillings and one sparrowhawk.

④ Leaving the **Angel**, retrace your steps as far as the church, and take the narrow side road (**School Lane**) immediately on its right. Follow this as it bends right and left to reach a T-junction; then turn right. After following this road for a little way, turn left again into a rough, stony lane. This soon reverts to a green lane, which, in turn, becomes a farm track leading into and over the Mill Field – one of the three fields included in Laxton's medieval open field system. Turn right on reaching the road, back to the visitor centre. (2¹/₂ miles)

 Date walk completed:

CONJURE ALDERS AND THE KING'S ROAD

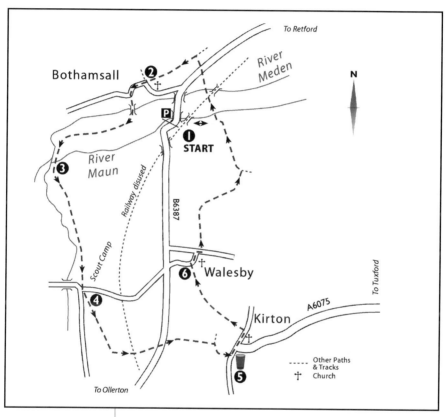

Distance:
10 miles

Starting point:
B6387 road,
Haughton, near
Bothamsall.
(Grid reference:
SK 681728)

Maps: OS Landranger 120 (Mansfield and Worksop)
OS Explorer 28 (270) (Sherwood Forest)

How to get there: From the A614 (Ollerton roundabout), follow the A6075 through New Ollerton, branching left at Boughton onto the B6387 and continuing via Walesby village. The parking area is just off the road on the second corner of a double bend.

ABOVE ROBIN HOOD'S CAVE, WALLESBY FOREST

*T*his walk embraces much history as we traverse wide open spaces and explore intimate woodland paths. And Bold Robin still lives – in spirit at least.

We start by following the River Maun for a short distance, before turning north and then west to reach the pretty village of Bothamsall. From here a long, straightish track takes us to Conjure Alders, where, for the briefest of trysts, the Maun and Meden flow as one. We continue along the King's Road, passing between the Maun on the one hand and Walesby Forest Scout Camp on the other. We then cross Boughton Brake and continue to the Fox, at Kirton.

Following our lunchtime break, we continue over the fields to Walesby village – where, if there is still time and you have a thirst on, you may wish to pause again for refreshment at the Red Lion – whence a series of clear tracks will lead us back to our starting point.

The Fox at Kirton (in Main Street) claims always to serve 'good beer and good cheer'. Kirton is not a big village, but the pub is busy and popular, with a ready welcome, a separate dining area, and an extensive open picnic area at the rear, as well as an intimate patio area, and a tempting play area (with bouncy castle when we called) for the children. The Fox is open from Monday to Friday between 12 noon and 3 pm and in the evenings from 6 pm till 11 pm. There is all-day opening at the weekend, from 12 noon until 11 pm on Saturday, and 10.30 pm on Sunday.

The menu is reasonably priced – and impressive, including such delicacies as 12-ounce sirloin steak, fresh poached salmon and 'Route 66' half-pound beefburgers. Authentic senior citizens can have a three-course lunch at a special price on Wednesday, while children have a menu of their own. Light bites include bangers and mash, cottage pie, omelettes and various hot and cold filled baguettes.

Telephone: *01623 860502*
*Alternative refreshment facilities will be found at the **Red Lion** in Walesby (telephone: 01623 861193).*

The Walk

① Leave the parking area and follow the track in an easterly direction, passing under the railway bridge and continuing along the field path beside the **River Maun**. Turn left to cross the river, passing **Haughton Hall Farm** and, for the second time, under the railway. From here, continue over the **River Meden** and cross the **B6387** to reach **Haughton Park House Farm**. Turn left here, following a green lane, and then the field path, to arrive at **Church Lane**, **Bothamsall**.
(1¹/₂ miles)

Bothamsall is peace. Coming here on a sunny Saturday in August, I saw few people, and those I did see were busily tending their pretty gardens. The village church is especially attractive when seen from the Church Lane approach – and almost equally so as viewed from the main street. Just outside the village on the Budby road is Bothamsall Castle – the remains of a motte and bailey structure believed to date back to the 12th century, and heavily embowered today in mature trees.

② Pass the church and continue straight ahead along **Main Street**, turning left at **Meadow Lane** and descending to re-cross the **Meden**.

After bending twice to the right, the track continues in a straight line for about ³/₄ mile to reach and follow the edge of a wood. Turn left with the track, now following a delightful footpath beside the **Meden** – flowing merrily down from a weir at **Conjure Alders**. Cross a footbridge (over the **Maun**), turning right then over slightly more difficult ground – overgrown and inclined to be wet – to reach (but not to cross) a second footbridge. (1¹/₂ miles)

Conjure Alders, strictly speaking, is the name of the woods at this point – which consist of a mix of ash and alder trees. The 'Conjure' element has nothing to do with sleight of hand, but is said to be a corruption of 'Coningswath', which was the Norse name for the crossing here, signifying the king's ford. And there was me, with my very limited knowledge of Latin and Norman French, thinking it meant a judicial gathering! The King's Road was an ancient way from Wellow to Blyth that followed the eastern boundary of the hunting forest, crossing the river at this point. It is here that the Maun and the Meden briefly combine forces; or so it appears from the map, and from the evidence on the ground.

③ Ignore this second footbridge and continue through the trees, following the '**Robin Hood Way**' route south,

CONJURE ALDERS

on the line of the former King's
Road. This develops into a lovely
woodland path, emerging eventually
onto open ground on the edge of
the **Walesby Forest Scout Camp**.
Turn right now and follow the
vehicle track along the perimeter of
the woods. This merges into a clear,
broad, sandy way along the western
edge of the camp site, with the
River Maun, initially screened from
sight, on your right. As the path
passes more closely to the river, an
excessively sandy little cliff-top will
be seen on the right. This is the site
of Robin Hood's Cave – a tiny
hideaway credited with having
sheltered the famous outlaw. This
stretch of the river bears the
alternative (and seemingly
inappropriate) name of Whitewater.
Continue along the edge of the
camping area to reach the road.
(1¼ miles)

*Walesby Forest is one of those
places that, once visited, never
lose their appeal. These 250 acres
of grass and woodland came into
the hands of the Nottinghamshire
Scout Association in 1938, thanks
to the generosity of the late
Colonel N. G. Pearson. Initially
reserved purely as a camp site,
the facilities have developed in
recent years beyond recognition,
with all manner of adventure
activities on offer, including
climbing, kayaking, traversing –
and frisbee golf! And guides can*

*camp here today, as well as their
brothers. It would be giving my
age away to say how long it is
since I first camped here – but it
was a very long time ago, when I
was still wet behind the ears. I
have been retired from Scouting
for quite a time now, but I still
retain my affection for 'Walesby –
Happy Land', a place full of
memories – some good, some less
so – the very stuff of life!*

④ Follow the road as far as the
junction, leaving here via a footpath
on the corner, to enter **Boughton
Brake**. The footpath crosses the
wood diagonally, keeping to the
same line throughout and emerging
eventually at a junction of tracks.
Turn left here, following **Brake Lane**
to the **B6387** road. Cross over to
join the farm track opposite, passing
through a hand-gate on the left and
turning right to follow the bridle-
path alongside the hedge. As the
field tapers down to a farm lane at
its far end, pass through the
gateway and cross a stile on the
right. Cross the field to reach
another gateway, passing through
and continuing on the right of the
hedge. In the next field, cross a stile
on the left and follow the hedge
line down the field to reach the
road (**A6075**) at **Kirton**. Turn
left for **the Fox**. (2¼ miles)

⑤ Follow the road north from the
pub, keeping left by the church

THE FOX AT KIRTON

along the minor road. A little way on, cross the stile on the left and descend the steps onto the field. The path from here crosses the field, bearing slightly to the right, and making directly for **Walesby** village, which should be visible in the distance. The path shows little if any evidence of regular use, but the stiles are sound and solid, and the waymarks clear. Turn right on reaching a green lane, and follow this into **Walesby** village.
(1 mile)

⑥ Continue along **Main Street**, turning right at the end (**Tuxford Road**); then left opposite the church onto **Green Lane**. Keep to this same track, going right and left with it and the ensuing footpath until you enter a farm lane, via a T-junction. Turn left here, continuing around a right-hand bend and beside a wood. The outward route is rejoined by **Haughton Hall Farm**. Turn left here, back to the car park.
($2^1/_2$ miles)

Date walk completed:

Walk 15

FOREST TRACKS AROUND MEDEN VALE AND CUCKNEY

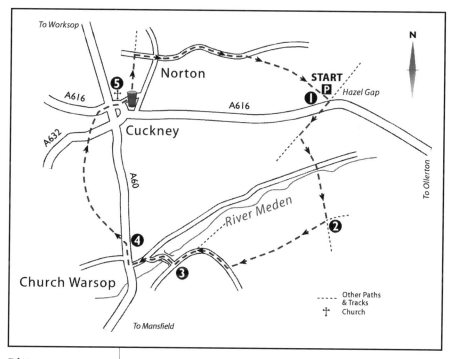

Distance:
8¹/₂ miles
Starting point:
Hazel Gap.
(Grid reference:
SK 599713)

Maps: OS Landranger 120 (Mansfield and Worksop)
OS Explorer 270 (28) (Sherwood Forest)

How to get there: Follow the A614 north from
Nottingham. At the Ollerton roundabout, take the second
exit – the A616 (Sheffield) road. Continue through Budby
and on for 1¹/₂ miles to Hazel Gap, where there is a small
off-road parking area in the woodland on the right.

THE GREENDALE OAK AT CUCKNEY IS A 17TH CENTURY COACHING INN

A superb walk this, which starts from a tiny half-concealed parking area on a busy forest road. Although Robin Hood passed on a long time ago, and the demands of the ensuing centuries have taken their inevitable toll on his former haunts, much of Sherwood Forest is still accessible to the adventurous rambler and most of the footpaths are good and clear. We plunge headlong into the forest – remaining there, and on the succeeding wide-open farmland, for the first three miles, during which you will be lucky (or not, as the case may be) if you meet another living soul. An enjoyable traverse of the Gleadthorpe forestlands is succeeded by a stretch of open country. While still conspiring to avoid excessive contact with our fellow persons, we make a brief return to the haunts of humankind by skirting around the former mining communities of Welbeck and Warsop, before continuing, by woodland and field path, to the welcoming village of Cuckney. The circle is completed by gentle walking over quiet roads and trails around Norton.

The Greendale Oak, in High Croft, Cuckney, is a charming 17th century grey stone coaching inn, with attractive drinking areas both inside and out, and accommodation for 60 persons in the non-smoking restaurant. There is a friendly welcome for all, including ramblers, cyclists, and families – and well-behaved dogs. Meals and bar snacks are served daily from 12 noon until 2 pm, and between 6 pm and 8.30 pm, or, at other times, by prior arrangement, and the house has a reputation for first class home cooked food. There is no printed menu, because the selection is changed on a regular basis, a wide range of delicacies being displayed on the blackboard. The pub is open all day every day – from 11.30 am until 11 pm Monday to Saturday, and 12 noon until 10.30 pm on Sundays. Bed and breakfast accommodation is available.

Telephone: *01623 844441*
*Alternative refreshment facilities are provided at **Jac's Café** in the centre of Cuckney; a pleasant picnic spot can be found by the Mill Pond at Church Warsop.*

 *The Walk*

where a grass path replaces the metalled way.
(1½ miles)

① From **Hazel Gap**, cross the road, and join a footpath which leaves the road here, travelling in a south-westerly direction along the inside edge of **Gleadthorpe Breck Plantation** and into the confusingly named **Gleadthorpe Plantation** – where the woodland is on both sides. Turn left at a guidepost, following the **Gleadthorpe** footpath. On reaching a lodge, cross the road and keep straight on, following the driveway over the **River Meden** and ascending gently. An alternative option is to transfer to the opposite (right-hand) side of the narrow belt of woodland,

② Turn right at an intersection and continue, still climbing easily along the perimeter of **Gleadthorpe New Plantation** and passing to the south of **Gleadthorpe Grange**.

There is no village of Gleadthorpe today, although there is said to have been such a settlement 'once upon a time', and traces of a Roman camp have been identified in the area. The name lives on in the various plantations and buildings hereabouts, especially in Gleadthorpe Grange, an agricultural research centre.

At the end of the woodland, continue ahead, following the edge of the fields and enjoying the wide-ranging views in every direction. Keep ahead along the farm track, ignoring an alternative track that leads off right. Bend right with the track on reaching a fenced enclosure (sewage works) – after pausing for a welcome rest on the bench at the bend. Continue down **Broomhill Lane**. (1½ miles)

③ Turn left at the road junction; then right opposite **Burns Farm**, following the road back over the **River Meden** and through a modern housing estate. Keep to the main estate road, continuing left at the Netherfield Lane junction, to reach the **A60** road junction and **Church Warsop**. (1 mile)

You might consider it worth your while to go to the left at the main road, just for a while, to enjoy the quiet beauty of this pretty spot on the River Meden, although it is not, strictly speaking, on our route. There is a fine big old church on the hill overlooking the village, and Warsop Mill, by the river, will amply repay a few minutes of your time, before you adjourn to the riverside – a delightful picnic

WARSOP MILL IS WORTH FINDING TIME TO INVESTIGATE

THE MILL POND AT CHURCH WARSOP

spot in its own right. This is 'Old Warsop' – as distinct from the busier former mining town of Market Warsop, just up the road. The village has lost a number of old structures over the past 50 years or so: a medieval packhorse bridge, an ancient dovecote and the former rectory – the haunt of a Roundhead soldier. There used to be a tradition in Warsop whereby the cottagers always left their street doors open – giving rise to the popular greeting to anyone with an open door: 'Do yo' come from Warsup?' Some say that they used to leave the doors open because they were more hospitable than the rest; others suggest that it was because they were more inquisitive. But that is not for you or me to judge!

④ Follow the **A60** north out of **Church Warsop**, passing the church and a road junction. Leave the road at a guidepost on your left (footpath to **Cuckney**), crossing several large arable fields and heading for the extreme left of a hilltop belt of woodland. Pass close to a power-line support post and enter the woodland (**Oakfield Plantation**), following the footpath inside the perimeter of the wood, as waymarked. Where the path branches, bear right a little and continue ahead, to emerge eventually onto open ground to the right of **Park House Farm**. Join the farm road and follow this down to the road (**A632**). Cross over and join a footpath, climbing steeply by steps and carrying on up and over to reach **School Lane**. Continue along the village street, crossing the **A60**, to reach the **Greendale Oak**. (2 miles)

Cuckney, an attractive little village, stands on the junction of three main roads which lead, spider fashion, in five separate directions. To the north lies the great ducal estate of Welbeck – a vast area of parkland, notably deficient in public footpaths and pubs – while to the south is the former mining community of Meden Vale – which gives a name to much of this area of forest and farm. It used to be called Welbeck Colliery Village, but about 30 years ago popular demand, I suppose, led to the adoption of a more agreeable name. Perhaps somebody had had a premonition, and heard the tolling of the bells for the coal industry.

⑤ Leave **Cuckney**, following **Norton Lane**. Pass the village church and, after crossing the **River Poulter**, take a footpath on the left. Follow the path over this first field, continuing round to the right and following the field edge to **Infield Lane**. Turn right along the road, following the **Robin Hood Way** left and right through **Norton** village and continuing on past **Bentinck Lodge**. Where the road bends left again, by **Corunna** Lodge, keep straight forward along the adjacent rough track, continuing on, through the woods, back to **Hazel Gap**. (2¹/₂ miles)

Date walk completed:

CLUMBER PARK AND ELKESLEY

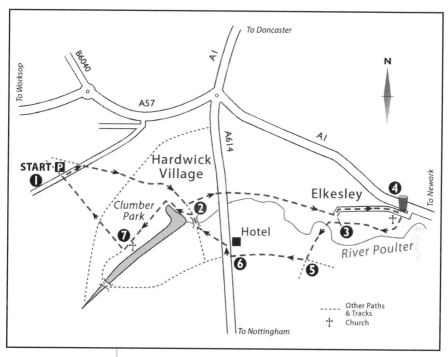

Distance:	**Maps:** OS Landranger 120 (Mansfield and Worksop)
12½ miles (or 10¼ miles)	OS Explorer 28 (270) (Sherwood Forest)

Starting point:
Forest Cottages
Plantation.
(Grid reference:
SK 611762)

How to get there: *From Apleyhead (at the junction of the A1 and the A614), follow the A57 west towards Worksop, turning left at the first junction (Manton Lodge) and continuing through the forest for about 1½ miles. The small parking area is on the right.*

THE FORD OVER THE RIVER POULTER AT ELKESLEY

*T*he National Trust has its East Midlands headquarters at Clumber, and the bulk of the surrounding parkland has been designated as a country park. Public rights of way abound and we are free to go almost anywhere we like, within reason, so throughout the duration of a longish walk we remain within the bounds of this great estate. We start out on the northern boundary of Clumber Park, our route taking us first through the wooded north-east area of the estate and across the impressive Lime Tree Avenue, bypassing for now the honeypot areas of lake and souvenir shop. After passing through Hardwick Village (the old staff estate), we cross the A614, following the long straight rural way to the village of Elkesley and our lunch spot. Our return route takes us over the charming River Poulter and along East Drayton Avenue – the old driveway road to Clumber. After recrossing the main road we re-enter Clumber Park, descending to join Clumber Lake at its foot, before continuing to the main complex of buildings, and thence to the car park.

The Robin Hood, in High Street, Elkesley, dates back in parts – so we are told – to the 15th or 16th century; but if you are expecting to find wild outlaws clad in Lincoln Green drinking here, or spit and sawdust on the floor, you will be disappointed. The atmosphere is a pleasant blend of traditional and modern, with a touch of style epitomised by the novelty of a bar counter which appears (erroneously, of course!) to have been fashioned out of a row of brassbound barrels. And then there are those traditional framed adverts upon the walls, for Reckitts Black Lead and Guinness – an interesting combination! The clientele is drawn from far and wide, attracted no doubt by the pub's reputation for fine cask ales and good food; a well-deserved reputation, as a quick glance at the comprehensive nature of the daily menu (varied every two or three weeks) will show. If ginger pig sausages, pan-fried supreme of chicken and mushrooms, or roast rack of English lamb fail to tempt your palate, why not try a poached fillet of smoked haddock – or sample something from the appetising range of light bites?

Lunchtime opening, in the week, is between 11.30 am and 3 pm; evenings from 6.30 pm till 11 pm; Sundays from noon until 2 pm and 7 pm till 10.30 pm. The dining area is non-smoking, but there is a separate bar area for smokers, as well as a beer garden. Dogs (well-behaved) are welcome, as also are families with children – for whom there is an outside play area.

Telephone: *01777 838259*
Light bar meals and snacks are also available at the **Clumber Park Hotel** *(Tavern Bar) on the main A614 road (telephone 01623 835333). The* **Clumber Park Tea Rooms** *provide refreshments too (telephone: 01909 544915).*

 *The Walk*

① Cross the road and take the trackway opposite, turning left after a few yards to follow a clear footpath running parallel to the road. Ignore a minor path which branches off to the right, and continue to a crossways. Turn right here, with the road to your rear, following the broad bridleway. Keep to the main track, ignoring any temptation to stray to the left, until you reach a stretch of more open ground and cross **Lime Tree Avenue**. Follow the road left a little here, to arrive at a guidepost on your right, indicating the resumed route of the bridleway. Follow this, branching left in due course at a blue bridleway arrow sign. The path climbs gently through the woods, crossing an intervening road and continuing to a second road junction. Turn right here, following the road to, and through, **Hardwick Village**, the private residential estate provided originally for the Clumber employees. (2 miles)

② Turn left beside the last of the houses, following a farm track and continuing up the ensuing slope and along the field-side footpath, with a wood on your right. Continue along a delightful woodland path, bearing right at a lesser junction to reach – and cross with extreme care – the **A614** road. A well-trodden footpath, initially enclosed, then leads onto fields. This path merges into a rough track, passing beneath two power lines, with the **River Poulter** very close – but well hidden – on the right. After passing through a block of woodland, the way continues, passing **Crookford Farm**, to meet the road at **Cross Lane**. (2¹/₂ miles)

Note: Those not wishing to visit **Elkesley** village and the **Robin Hood** inn can shorten their journey by 2¹/₄ miles by turning right at this point to reach and cross the **River Poulter**, continuing from there to **West Drayton Avenue**, as described below in stage 4 of the walk. (³/₄ mile)

③ To reach **Elkesley**, turn left and then right at **Coalpit Lane**, continuing ahead past the church to

reach the **Robin Hood** on the left. (1 mile)

The village of Elkesley is almost cut off from the outside world today, surprisingly perhaps, by the main A1 road. When the first edition of the 1-inch Ordnance Survey map of this area was published in 1840, the village possessed all the usual connections to the villages on every side. In the meantime, the Great North Road has been realigned and – as a consequence, Elkesley's only escape route, by road, is onto the A1. However, it is a two-edged sword, as the absence of any through traffic makes the village road a great deal safer. All that apart, it is a nice, tidy little village, and not what you would call sleepy. It has a fine church, a pretty river, a good pub, its own school and a thriving community of traditional and modern houses. What more could you ask?

④ Leaving the pub, cross the road and follow **Low Road**, turning right at the end onto **Brough Lane**. The village centre is soon left behind, and pleasant views open up on our left, over **Crookford Hill** and towards the distant woods, as we proceed. On reaching a gated enclosure, keep to the right between the fences, continuing along a metalled access road and turning left on the second bend to reach the

River Poulter, crossed via a long wooden footbridge. Over the bridge, continue ahead over more open ground, keeping straight ahead on a lesser track where the way branches. Keep on through the woods and over the ensuing fields to reach an unfenced road (**West Drayton Avenue**). (2 miles)

West Drayton Avenue today is little more – at any point – than a long distance farm access road. In places, it is simply a very useful footpath. But its straight nature and its starting and finishing points clearly emphasise its origins: as a driveway linking Clumber House with the Great North Road.

⑤ Turn right. The metalled road soon reverts to a rough, unmade track, to remain so for much of the way before becoming a simple, but highly satisfactory, footpath. After rejoining a farm track, leave this on a bend, crossing a stile and turning right onto the **A614**, to reach the **Clumber Park Hotel** (**Dukeries Tavern**). (1¼ miles)

⑥ Cross the road – again with care – and enter the gateway. After a short distance, a footpath branches off right, crossing the fields. I suspect there is usually a good view down to the lake from here, but I didn't see it, as the whole of this vast acreage – apart from the excellent footpath – was taken up by an eight-foot tall crop of lupins! Reaching a road, turn right and cross the **River Poulter** – again via a

THE ROBIN HOOD AT ELKESLEY CAN BE TRACED BACK TO THE 15TH CENTURY

footway, unless you prefer to risk wetting your feet by using the ford. Bear left after passing a farm on your left, crossing a parking area to reach the foot of the lake. Turn right, following the lake side to its extreme end, and cross the footway, continuing straight on ahead. On reaching a 'trefoil' junction, turn left and continue to the main buildings complex. (2¹/₄ miles)

We do not have many National Trust properties in Nottinghamshire, but Clumber – the Regional Headquarters – makes up for the deficit. The estate consists of 3,800 acres of woods, parkland, heath and farmland, with a superb lake as the crowning jewel; all of this constitutes just one portion of the once flourishing 'Dukeries' of Nottinghamshire. Clumber House was built by the Duke of Newcastle in 1770, and

demolished in 1938. The beautiful church, more recently built, remains, as do many of the original buildings and the handsome Clumber Bridge – and the 'Duke's Drive', Lime Tree Avenue. The park itself is always open, although the various additional facilities – gardens, chapel, conservation centre, shop and refreshments – are open at certain times only. (General enquiries – telephone: 01909 544917)

⑦ From the buildings complex, turn right and follow the road past the parking area, keeping to the left of the cricket field and ignoring all right turns for the present. Cross **Lime Tree Avenue** and bear right along the footpath, continuing back to your starting point. (1¹/₂ miles)

Date walk completed:

SPALFORD WARREN, NORTH AND SOUTH CLIFTON

THE RED LION INN AT SOUTH CLIFTON

Distance:
9 miles

Starting point:
Spalford Warren
Nature Reserve.
(Grid reference:
SK 834681)

Maps: OS Landranger 121 (Lincoln and Newark-on-Trent)
OS Explorer 271 (Newark-on-Trent)

How to get there: *From Newark, follow the A46 north-east, turning left onto the A1133 (Gainsborough road) and continuing north through Collingham and Besthorpe. Turn right about 3 miles further on, to Spalford. Turn right again in the village (Rabbithill Lane), keeping straight on where the road bends left, to follow the unmade road into Spalford Warren Nature Reserve.*

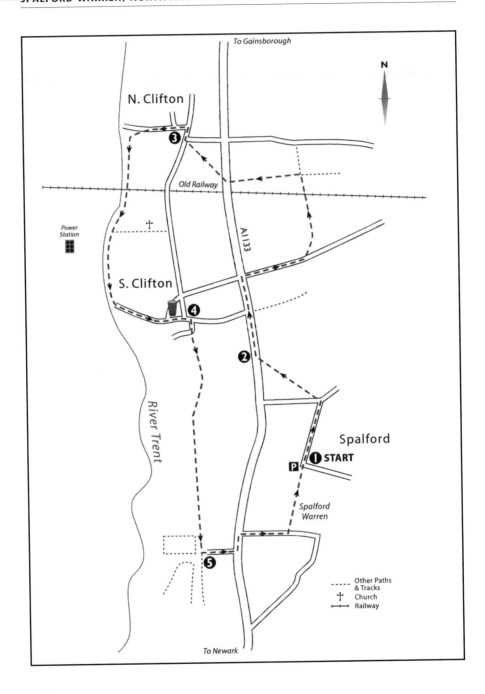

*W*e start out from the Spalford Warren Nature Reserve, following a meandering route by road, footpath and country lane, to North Clifton, where the star attraction is the beautiful Japanese garden created by one of our county's welcome guests, the Buddha Maitreya. From here, we follow the riverside path and are reminded of the might of Britain's power industry as we contemplate the cooling towers of High Marnham Power Station on the opposite bank. The river takes us to South Clifton and a welcome lunch break. We complete the circle along field paths and rural lanes, over land touched, but not unduly scarred, by gravel workings.

The Red Lion Inn, on High Street, South Clifton, is an attractive 19th century free house which retains its traditional character, with beamed ceilings, an open fireplace and tasteful décor and furnishings. The atmosphere is busy and friendly. Lunchtime opening on Friday is from 12 noon until 2.30 pm and on Saturday and Sunday from 12 noon until 3 pm. The 'Lion' does not open at lunchtime on the other days, but special arrangements, including provision of food, can be made for parties of walkers if arranged in advance. Evening opening is from 5.30 pm to 11 pm Monday to Friday; 6 pm to 11 pm on Saturday; 7 pm to 10.30 pm on Sunday.

Food is likewise served at lunchtime from Friday to Sunday; also every evening from 6 pm (7 pm on Sunday) till 9 pm. The menu caters for all tastes – including, for the very hungry, the American dream – consisting of a full rack of hickory smoked ribs in a barbecue sauce, and a butterfly cajun chicken breast. If, on the other hand, you prefer something more traditionally English, you could go for sausage and mash or cod and chips with mushy peas. There is a pleasing selection of lunchtime light bites at reasonable prices, as well as a special menu for children. Real ales include Home Bitter and two guest ales; these change on a weekly basis.

Telephone: *01522 778 660*
Light refreshments are available (if visiting the gardens) at
*the **Pureland Japanese Garden** in North Clifton. Open every day*
except Monday.

The Walk

① Follow the lane out of the nature reserve, continuing north along the road to **Spalford** village. On reaching **Sand Lane** – the main street – turn left briefly, then right at a farm entrance. Cross a stile on the left of the drive, passing through a thicket and continue, half right, over two fields. In the far corner of the second field, pass through the gap and turn left to follow the hedge to the top of the field and round to a stile, which leads out to a redundant section of old roadway now bypassed. Join the main road (**A1133**) and turn right. (1¼ miles)

Spalford Warren Nature Reserve occupies 26.5 hectares of woodland and blown sand heath, and is a Site of Special Scientific Interest in the care of the Nottinghamshire Wildlife Trust. The name of the site and its location on Rabbithill Lane suggest that the land was once used in the rearing of rabbits. In more recent times it was used as a munitions dump – but there is little if anything now to indicate that.

Apart from patches of heather, gorse and broom, a number of more specialised sand-land plants can be found here, such as shepherd's cress and field mouse-ear. Various bird and animal species have been recorded, including sparrowhawk, woodpeckers, woodcock, sand wasps and lizards.

② Follow the road for ½ mile or so, taking advantage of the wide grass verge. In doing so, you are asked to bear in mind that this is a designated wildlife verge and to have appropriate respect for the wildlife interest. Passing the first turning on the left, which leads to **South Clifton**, continue to the next turning – a crossroads – and turn right towards **Wigsley**. Turn left again after a further ½ mile, following an enclosed farm lane (**Wheatholme Lane**). After crossing a disused railway turn left at a crossways to follow **Moor Lane**. On reaching the **A1133** road again, cross over, turning half right to cross two fields. Pass through a gap in the hedge line, following the top edge of the third field, with houses visible ahead. Cross a stile and continue, again half left, to reach a stile beside a farm gate leading out to the road at **North Clifton**. Turn right initially, then left at the road junction to reach **Pureland**. (2¾ miles)

The Buddha Maitreya was born in Japan where, while he was still in his teens, a search for religious truth led him first to Christianity. He failed to find there the enlightenment he sought, however, so turned to meditation and, in due course, to an MA degree in Buddhist Theology. He later visited Thailand, India and Nepal and, ultimately, England, where he spent time teaching and lecturing at various universities. He came to North Clifton in 1973, taking over a derelict two-acre plot of land as a base for teaching meditation. And so was born the Pureland Relaxation and Meditation Centre.

③ It would be a great pity to leave **North Clifton** without first spending an hour or so at **Pureland**, enjoying the beauty and tranquillity of the Japanese Garden created by

Maitreya – a man with no previous gardening experience, but a wealth of dedication – out of a bare plot of land. Leaving **North Clifton**, follow **Trent Lane** down to the riverside, turning left here and continuing along the top of the flood bank, on the line of the **Trent Valley Way**.

The view over the river here is dominated by the bulk of High Marnham Power Station with its complement of massive cooling towers. The Trent Valley has been called the 'Power House of England', High Marnham being just one in a string of similar structures erected along its banks in the past 50 years or so. Like

NEAR GIRTON

the more modern hilltop batteries of wind turbines, they perform an essential service.

Turn left onto another **Trent Lane** and continue to **South Clifton** village and the **Red Lion Inn**. (2¹/₄ miles)

The villages of North and South Clifton, although separated one from the other by a mile of road, are in many respects a single community. They share a church and a school, both of which are situated midway between the two. Apart from these, both villages used to be self-sufficient, each with its own full complement of trades and professions. Most of these have now gone, as has the South Clifton ferry, which the North Clifton people were able to use for free, provided they supplied the ferryman with a prime loaf on Christmas Day.

Rugby Union buffs will be interested to know, incidentally, that South Clifton is the home of the great 'Dusty' Hare, MBE.

④ Turn left out of the pub, following **Vicarage Road**; then right at the next road junction. Where the road bends right by some farm buildings, keep straight on ahead along the green lane, ascending **Clifton Hill**. The track bends left at the top of the hill – but ignore this, again keeping straight on down the slope to reach a stile and footbridge in the far corner of the field. Cross the footbridge and continue beside the hedge, crossing two successive fields and a stream. The path then adopts a straight course, entering a broad farm lane. After passing beneath a power line, continue past a former gravel pit, now a scenic pond, and turn left into **Meadow Lane**. (1³/₄ miles)

⑤ Turn left at the **A1133** road; then right again at **Green Lane**. Continue past the first entrance to **Spalford Warren** and a large farm building on the right to reach **Rabbithill Lane** (unsurfaced track). Turn left here, back to the parking area. (1 mile)

Date walk completed:

110

THE IDLE WAY
FROM SUTTON
TO RETFORD

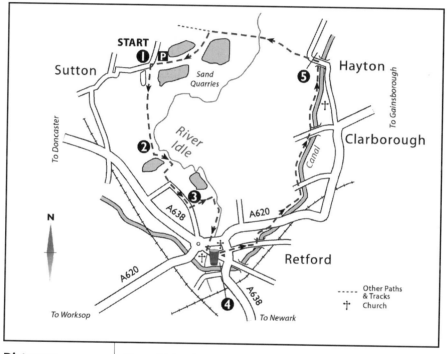

Distance:	Maps: OS Landranger 120 (Mansfield and Worksop)
10½ miles	OS Explorer 271 (Newark-on-Trent) and 279 (Doncaster)

Starting point:
Lound Low Road, Sutton cum Lound. (Grid reference: SK 692851)

How to get there: *From the A1 at Apleyhead (south-east of the A614 junction) follow the B6420 north-east. Cross the A620, continuing via unclassified roads and crossing the A638. Turn right in Sutton village, following Lound Low Road. Where the road turns sharp left, keep straight ahead on the unmetalled road, as for the Wetlands Waterfowl Reserve, and park as soon as convenient.*

THE WETLANDS NATURE RESERVE, SUTTON CUM LOUND

Sutton cum Lound, where this walk begins, is right out in the sticks, in sand and gravel country, but close enough to Retford for the mileage to be counted on the fingers of one hand. We are never far from water here, as we walk alongside the various ponds and lakes resulting from the worked out pits, and follow, for much of the way to Retford, the course of the River Idle – which wanders pleasantly and peacefully along towards the Trent, playing host to mallard, swan, moorfowl and Canada goose, and never quite living up to its indolent name. The Idle begins life as the Maun and the Meden, which flirt with one another all the way from Mansfield and Warsop in the west to West Drayton, near Retford, where they finally plight their troth to continue as one river. We pause for refreshment in Retford town before forsaking the river in favour of the Chesterfield Canal, following the Cuckoo Way to Hayton, from where we strike across country, passing over the River Idle for the last time, to reach the Wetlands Waterfowl Reserve.

The Turk's Head, in Grove Street, Retford, was built as recently as 1938, a truth belied by the traditional appearance of the half timbered, local stone exterior. The oak panelled interior is just as attractive, and the warm demeanour of the management and clientele perfects the welcoming atmosphere.

In this Pubmaster's house, lunchtime opening is from 11 am to 3 pm (4 pm on Saturday) and between 7 pm and 11 pm in the evenings (10.30 pm on Sunday). Food is available lunchtimes only, between 12 noon and 2.30 pm. The menu carries an impressive range of mouth-watering dishes, all at reasonable prices, including a selection of main courses, with a choice of chipped, new or jacket potatoes. Yorkshire puddings, sandwiches and rolls, daily specials and home-made puddings and pies are also included – and the landlord's Italian lasagne is celebrated throughout the district. A wide range of traditional hand-pulled and guest ales is on offer, including Adnams, Tetleys and Theakstons. Bed and breakfast accommodation can be provided.

Telephone: *01777 702742*
Alternative refreshment facilities will be found at the **Gate Inn**, *Clarborough (telephone: 01777 703397 and at the* **Boat Inn**, *Hayton (telephone 01777 700158).*

The Walk

① Retrace your way to the road junction, and leave the road on the bend, following a waymarked footpath in a southerly direction along the edge of **Sutton Lake**. Most of the former pits, including this one, have now been adopted as fishing lakes – controlled, rather oddly (like those we found near Hoveringham) by the Derbyshire County Angling Club.

It appears, from a notice part way along the path, that adders have been seen in the vicinity of Sutton Lake. The adder, or viper, is Britain's only venomous snake, and its bite can be fatal to humans. Having said that, it would be a rare thrill to catch a glimpse of this elusive reptile as it dashes for cover at the approach of human feet. I myself have been rambling regularly for many years – including, in the course of my research, three times along this particular section of the walk – and have yet to meet an adder. But there is always a first time. Wise council is to keep your eyes skinned and watch where you are putting your feet, especially on the sandier ways, and along the more overgrown footpaths.

After leaving the lakeside, the way continues along an enclosed section of path and through a light metal hand-gate to meet a farm track. On the OS map the footpath is shown as continuing through the woodland to the left of the track. There does not appear, however, to be any access into the woods at this point, and I am advised that it is acceptable to follow the track. At the end of the track, pass through a gateway and turn left, looking for a fragmentary path, which is reached

in a short distance, on the right. Follow this one through to the **River Idle**, and turn right again. After following the river for a short distance, the track crosses a quarry road with private quarry areas on both sides. Cross a stile on the right and continue along the wooded footpath, ignoring a couple of footpath signs on your left. On reaching a fence and stile, ignore these too, and turn left, to cross a footbridge and reach the **Hallcroft** fishing lake. (1¼ miles)

② Turn left, following the lakeside path around the head of the lake and rejoining the **River Idle**. The

THE TURK'S HEAD, RETFORD, WAS BUILT IN 1938

lake is massive and beautiful, and the path between it and the river is a constant delight, with anglers and waterfowl providing a diverting accompaniment to the walk. It is technically possible to continue beside the river all the way through to **Retford**, and there appears to be a clear and open way through, but this next section has not, at the time of writing, been dedicated as a public right of way. For this reason, you should continue along the footpath around the third side of the lake to join a road and turn left. The road here has been blocked off to traffic, but a way through will be found for tramps like us, via the opposite hedge. Continue down **Hallcroft Road**, passing the recycling centre, and the **Flying Scotsman** inn and turning left onto **Camborne Crescent**. (1¹/₂ miles)

③ Follow the road through the housing estate and through a field gate, continuing on over the fields to rejoin the river. Do not cross the footbridge, but turn right, following the riverside path through to Retford. Pass under the A620, emerging onto Bridgegate, and turn left. Follow the road right and left round the square and continue along Grove Street to the Turk's Head inn. (1³/₄ miles)

④ This is one of those walks where all the real adventure is got through before lunch. So you can now relax

and enjoy the long, but easy stroll along the **Cuckoo Way** (see Walk 20). Continue on along **Grove Road**, crossing **Arlington Way** to reach the **Chesterfield Canal** at **Grove Mill**. Follow the canal path left, passing beneath **Leverton Road** and the **A620** and continuing via **Whitsunday Pie Lock** and **Clarborough**, to **Hayton**. Enjoy it. There is not much to disturb your peace; a boat or two if you are lucky, a scattering of wildfowl, an occasional angler and, perhaps, a few booted and knapsacked kindred spirits with whom to compare notes. There are a couple of good pubs too along the way, if you develop a thirst. My own special treat was to see the Red Arrows fly over en route to or from some festival or fete. (3¹/₂ miles)

⑤ Leave the canal at **Hayton**, following the road west as far as the first bend, where the way continues ahead along a byway (**Chain Bridge Lane**). This is a quiet and peaceful old road, crossing the wide open arable and sandy spaces between **Hayton** and **Lound**. You are unlikely to meet anyone or anything for at least the first mile. Soon after crossing the **River Idle**, take a side turning, by the active quarry lands, onto **Lound Low Road**.

There is something secretive about the sand quarrying industry. Despite all the evidence of past and present working in this area, the only confirmation I have come across of actual industry (apart from the occasional truckload of sand, or men in hard hats) is the sight and sound of the conveyor belts. These intriguing

HALLCROFT FISHERIES

features, of minimal width and depth, and containing a mere trickle of moist golden sand, seem to run for miles along the perimeter of the workings, carefully tunnelling beneath the roadways and elaborately negotiating bends in their chosen course. Where they begin and end is a mystery. Perhaps they just circulate in a never-ending spiral to disappear who knows where?

Continue along Lound Low Road, passing **Sutton Grange Farm** and

continuing back to the **Waterfowl Reserve**. (2¹/₂ miles)

Before returning home, why not call in for a while at the Waterfowl Reserve? Despite its title, there is an infinite variety of exotic fauna here apart from the waterfowl – peacocks, snowy owls, turkey vultures, marmosets, prairie dogs and wallabies to name but a few – not to mention a fair number of Homo sapiens piscatoriensis: fishermen to you. Refreshments are also available.

Date walk completed:

LANGOLD, BLYTH AND HODSOCK

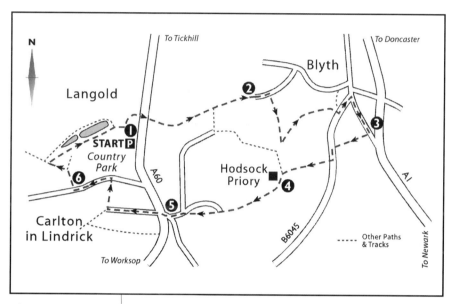

Distance:
10 miles
Starting point:
Langold Country Park (Grid reference: SK 582864). A parking fee may be levied, depending on the season.

Maps: OS Landranger 120 (Mansfield and Worksop)
OS Explorer 279 (Doncaster)

How to get there: Follow the A60 north from Worksop for 5 miles, passing through Carlton in Lindrick. Turn left after the Cosford Industrial Estate to reach the main car park.

THE PATH NEAR HODSOCK

*T*he walking in this area, right on the frontier between Nottinghamshire and South Yorkshire (we actually trespass briefly on the wrong side of the border!), as in so much of the county, is easy and relaxing, over broad arable acres with no hills of any consequence, but long views nevertheless. This walk starts from the Langold Country Park, but we do not linger here, preferring to defer that pleasure until the end of the walk. A gentle stroll along quiet byways – plus a brief but adventurous spell tracing an ill-defined field path – brings us to our lunch venue at Blyth. We continue to Hodsock Hall, where, at the right time of the year, we can pause awhile to enjoy the famous display of snowdrops. Then on, via Carlton in Lindrick, back to Langold – and a stroll beside beautiful Langold Lake.

The White Swan, on Blyth's Main Street, is over 200 years old and one of the oldest inns in the area. Sandwiched between its neighbours and looking out over the charming green, the narrow frontage is liable to mislead, the interior being surprisingly spacious, with an intriguing arrangement of interconnecting rooms grouped around the single bar counter. The blend of old red brick and traditional timber conveys an impression of age – as does the unusual free-standing brick-built fireplace in the centre of the main bar area. This is an Enterprise Inns house, open daily between 12 noon and 2.30 pm; and in the evening from 7 pm until 11 pm.

Food is served – full meals as well as bar snacks – every day from 12 noon until 2 pm, and in the evening – except Sunday – between 7 pm and 9 pm. Fish is a speciality here; so too is the beef and ale pie; plus, of course, you will find daily specials. And the traditional Sunday roast. If you are looking for a delicious dessert, I can recommend the home-made apple and elderberry pie. Real ales include John Smith's and Whitbread's Trophy Bitter.

Telephone: *01909 591222*
*Alternative refreshment facilities can be found at the **Inn on the Park** in Langold Country Park. Or you may prefer to picnic by the lake.*

The Walk

① Follow the country park access road back to the **A60**. There are refuges just a short distance along the road to left and to right, one or other of which you are recommended to use, for your own safety, in crossing over to join the farm road opposite. Keep to the farm road for about 1½ miles, ignoring all side turnings and continuing straight on ahead as the metalled road gives way to an unsurfaced farm track. (1¾ miles)

② After passing **Hodsock Cottage**, the road is again surfaced. Continue past a triangular plantation; then turn right through a farm gate, this being the logical alternative to a nearby stile, which appears to have been abandoned to nature. Walk straight down the field, with the hedge on your right, turning right through the gap at the far end and then left through a second gap, and continuing, again down the field, but this time with the hedge on your left. About three parts of the way down this long field, pass through a gap on your left; then double back half-left to cross two fields on a diagonal line. Cross the ditch (in the bottom of which is a boundary stone) and turn right.

Continue through a wood and over the **River Ryton**; then on over two fields – intersected by a green lane – to reach a track running left to right. Turn right here, then left at the road (**B6045**) to reach **Main Street** in **Blyth** and the **White Swan**. (2 miles)

The big village – or small town? – of Blyth has a long tradition of hospitality and an honourable history that dates back over 900 years. The Norman overlord of Tickhill, Sir Roger de Builli, chose Blyth as the site for a Benedictine Priory, which flourished in the early Middle Ages. There were two leper hospitals here as well in those days, one of which still stands, having served in more recent years as the village school and an army canteen. The second hospital has gone, but its site is still recognisable in Spital Farm, through which our walk will continue.

Blyth has always been popular with visitors, and with travellers along the Great North Road. Having said which, the modern bypass has done much to preserve the character of the village, and saved it from complete mayhem!

③ Leaving the **White Swan**, follow

THE GATEHOUSE OF HODSOCK PRIORY

Main Street south, continuing as far as the **A1 slip road**. Turn right here to follow the farm road past **Spital Farm**. Turn left at the road (**Briber Hill**); then right again at the next junction, re-crossing the **River Ryton** and continuing to **Hodsock Priory**. (1³/₄ miles)

Hodsock Priory is a misnomer, for there never was a priory here. Its proper name, until the end of the 19th century, was simply Hodsock, or Hodsock Hall, and its history extends back long before the Norman Conquest. The site was occupied in the Bronze Age and in Roman times, and relics of those periods are still found here from time to time. Hodsock was the property of the Clifton family for fourteen generations, before passing by sale, in 1765, to the Mellish family, from whom the current owner, Sir Andrew Buchanan, is descended.

The present house was built in the 19th century, on the site of an earlier manor house, but the impressive gatehouse – a Grade 1 listed building – dates back to the end of the 15th century. The gardens are particularly beautiful, especially in February, when visitors flock here from far and wide to admire the stunning display of snowdrops.

④ Swing left with the track, passing **Hodsock Priory Farm**; then turn right, with a row of large barns on your left and the gardens on your right. The road becomes a rough track from here on, passing a series of horse paddocks and continuing over the fields towards **Carlton in Lindrick**. This is very peaceful, level and pretty country, best enjoyed at a leisurely pace! After an unfenced crossing of two large fields, the track bends right. Cross a stile here, on the left, and continue via the field path, with the hedge on your right and the outskirts of **Carlton** now visible in the distance. Continue along an enclosed footpath to the road and turn right, passing **The Green** and following the road round to reach the **A60** (**Doncaster Road**). (1¹/₂ miles)

Carlton in Lindrick used to be known as the 'Rose Village', but was also famous as the home of the Carlton Daffodil. Before the 1939-45 war, the local Ramsden family used to invite the children of the neighbourhood round to their home at Wigthorpe Hall to pick the daffodils – which they did with gay abandon, carrying the flowers home in great armfuls. The village has seen a number of changes in the course of the 20th century. Originally a mainly agricultural settlement with few modern amenities, the sinking of the nearby Firbeck Colliery in the 1920s brought new opportunities to the local workforce. Today, the pit is gone and many of the locals commute elsewhere.

⑤ Cross **Doncaster Road** and turn left, then immediately right to follow **Long Lane** (which it is!). At the top of the lane turn right onto a footpath passing to the rear of the houses, with open fields on your left. Turn left again on reaching a road and pass an industrial depot, continuing along the road to reach **Buckwood Farm**. (1$^1/_2$ miles)

⑥ Turn right here, and follow the farm track past the buildings. This is where we cheat a little by straying into South Yorkshire – but only for a matter of $^1/_2$ mile or so. The county boundary is crossed as we approach a stile, which we also cross, leaving the farm track then and turning left to cross a second stile and continue over a large arable field, making towards the woods on the far side. Do not cross the woods, but turn right on reaching them, following the edge of the field and continuing beside the upper lake. You might find the perfect spot for a picnic here; I did! On reaching the main lake (and re-entering Nottinghamshire), you have a choice of routes back to the car park: along either the north or the south bank of the lake. I took the southern one, which is probably the more convenient for the main car park. You can, of course, follow the path all the way round if you wish – bearing in mind that you will still have to get back to the car park afterwards! (1$^1/_2$ miles)

Langold Country Park was originally designed in the early 19th century as a formal estate. A hall was planned to be built on the northern bank of the lake, but this never reached fruition. The park is very popular in the summer and at bank holiday times, when a modest parking fee may be charged. Facilities include a cricket field, bowling green, bandstand and refreshment facilities, which include the Inn on the Park, formerly the Cosford Colliery Miners' Welfare. Fishing is possible in the lake and there is also a wealth of wildlife, particularly bird life, on the lake and in the various wooded areas.

Date walk completed:

LANCASTER LOVERS AND CLAYWORTH CUCKOOS

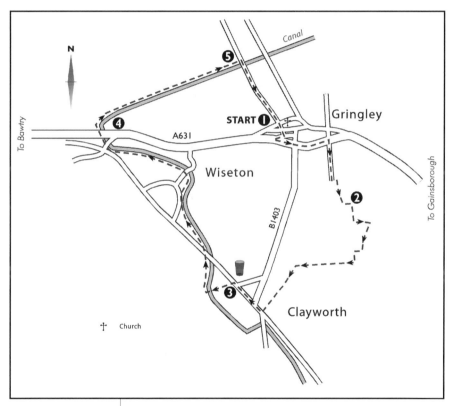

Distance:
9¹/₂ miles

Starting point:
High Street,
Gringley on the Hill.
(Grid reference:
SK 735906)

Maps: OS Landranger 112 (Scunthorpe)
OS Explorer 280 (Isle of Axholme)

How to get there: *Follow the A631 (Gainsborough road) from Bawtry, passing Everton and bearing left at the second Gringley on the Hill turning. Keep straight ahead at a road junction and park on the roadside (High Street).*

GRINGLEY TOP LOCK

*T*here is a lot to commend this region to the discriminating wanderer: broad acres, pleasant and quiet villages, peaceful easy walking, distant views. And are you, like me, fascinated by the infinite variety of curious and unusual names attached by mankind to his local roads and ways? If you are, then this walk should please you. We begin by following Lancaster Road, which is nowhere near Lancaster, continuing along Lovers' Lane, and a part of the Trent Valley Way that is miles from the river. After calling in for refreshment at Clayworth, on the line of the Lincoln to Doncaster Roman road, the remainder of our journey follows the Cuckoo Way – aka the Chesterfield Canal towpath.

When I surveyed this walk on a hot June day the undergrowth and overgrowth on the little-used country paths were rampant. But there were many compensations. The ducklings on the canal were delightful; the wild flowers were glorious; and the solitude was absolute. Lesson: take it as it comes; but be prepared – and don't adopt the new fashion of walking 'au naturel'!

The Blacksmith's Arms, in Town Street, Clayworth, is an attractive 17th century free house providing a warm welcome to families and loners – and to walkers (but any muddy boots should be removed and left in the porch). Full bar meals and bar snacks are available daily from 12 noon until 2 pm; also between 6 pm (7 pm on Sunday) and 9.30 pm. A comprehensive menu, including such delicacies as escalope of Scotch salmon, grilled roast shoulder of lamb, and char-grilled gammon steak, is listed on the bar blackboard, and there is also a full range of grills, ploughman's lunches and sandwiches and a special children's menu. And if you are looking for a classier meal out, why not visit the integral Wiseton Restaurant?

Telephone: *01777 818171*
Alternative refreshment facilities are available at the **Brewer's Arms***, also on Clayworth's Town Street (telephone 01777 816107), or at the* **White Swan** *at Drakeholes (telephone 01777 817206).*

① Cut through to the main road (**A631**) and cross over, turning left towards **Gainsborough**. Ignore a road signposted for Clayworth, and a footpath just beyond, continuing to the next turning – **Lancaster Road** – and turning right. After an initial straight stretch of metalled road, the way reverts to a tortuously winding unmade lane edged with, among other flora, wild rose, cow parsley and brambles. Enjoy the distant arable views – and the birdsong, which, when I came, included a chorus of skylarks and a distant woodpigeon or two. (1½ miles)

② Where the track fades out in a field, continue beside the hedge and turn right at the end to follow the waymarked footpath along the field's edge. Turn left at the top of the field and continue until you reach a footbridge on the right, leading into a belt of woodland. Follow the footpath through the wood, emerging at length into an overgrown green lane and turning right. Go to the left in the field for a short distance only, after which a footpath will be seen emerging through the hedge to cross from left to right. Turn right here, crossing two long fields and continuing along another green lane. At the end, pass through the farm gate and turn left into **Toft Dyke Lane**, continuing through to **Clayworth** village. Turn right for the **Blacksmith's Arms**. (2¼ miles)

DRAKEHOLES BASIN

Clayworth lies on the B1403 Lincoln to Doncaster Roman road. A pleasant, quiet linear village, it has a hall, a manor house, and a fine old church, parts of which date back at least as far as the 12th century. Back in 1655 the living was presented by the Protector, Oliver Cromwell, to his namesake John Cromwell, of Barnby Moor; not for any reasons of kinship but, apparently, just on account of having the same name! This Cromwell appears to have enjoyed mixed fortunes, for he fell from favour in 1662 on suspicion of plotting against the government.

There are two pubs – the Blacksmith and the Brewer both have their arms here – and a scattering of red-brick homes. The Chesterfield Canal loops around the village, and the moorings of the Retford and Worksop Boat Club are here. One of the canal crossings, which we shall use later, is by Otters' Bridge. The name has nothing to do with small aquatic animals, but commemorates the Otter family, long-term owners of Royston Manor.

③ Leaving the **Blacksmith's Arms**, follow the adjacent footpath over the fields to join a farm lane,

126

turning left. Cross **Otter Bridge** and turn right along the canal towpath. Pass under **Gray's Bridge** and carry on via the hamlet of **Wiseton** and **Lady's Bridge** to **Drakeholes Tunnel**. (2³/₄ miles)

The Chesterfield Canal was opened in 1777, linking the industrial areas of the Nottinghamshire/ Derbyshire border with the River Trent at West Stockwith. As with so many other canals, however, the Chesterfield was seriously affected by the coming of the railways, although it did manage to survive intact until 1907, when

THE BLACKSMITH'S ARMS AT CLAYWORTH

the Norwood Tunnel, between Chesterfield and Worksop, collapsed. The Nottinghamshire section remained navigable by commercial traffic until the 1950s. That the canal is now navigable again over most of its length is due largely to the campaigning efforts of the Retford and Worksop Boat Club. The towpath is open to walkers throughout its 46-mile length – and goes by the intriguing title of the Cuckoo Way. It seems that, when the canal boats were first introduced to the canal in the 18th century, the river boatmen on the Trent described them as cuckoos – and the canal as the Cuckoo Dyke.

In the 19th century, the hamlet of Wiseton was the home of Lord Althorpe, who was later created Earl Spencer and who died here at Wiseton in 1845. Drakeholes, close by, is even smaller; but it occupies an enviable position on a junction of roads and boasts a hotel, a farm and the canal basin and tunnel – and an attractive name. A small Roman station is believed to have stood on the spot.

④ Join the road at **Drakeholes Basin**, following round to the right of the **White Swan Hotel** and ignoring the first road turning on the left. Leave via the farm track close by, continuing up and over and keeping to the left, to rejoin the canal path where the tunnel ends. The canal bends sharply to the right, after which it continues on a straight course, providing a peaceful, leisurely walk all the way through to **Gringley Lock**. (2 miles)

⑤ Join the road at **Gringley Lock**, turning right and continuing up the hill to **Gringley High Street**. (1 mile)

Although it is not what you would call a big hill, the ground to the north of Gringley declines determinedly to the fenland of Misterton Car and the River Idle, lending weight to the suggestion that the Minsters of York and Beverley, as well as Lincoln Cathedral, can be seen from here. Saxon and Danish remains have been found, but tradition suggests that, even before these, Gringley

Hill served as a lookout point for the Britons. A sizeable village, Gringley has always had a rebellious streak. Of the four bells in the parish church tower, one is said to date from the Commonwealth period, when such items as bells were considered frivolous. A later vicar – one Gustavus Hopton Scott – refused to accept the authority of the newly formed diocese of Southwell and insisted on maintaining his allegiance to Lincoln. A man of independent opinions, Scott refused to tolerate interference from anyone – including diocesan officials – and is said to have seen off all unwelcome visitors with a loaded shotgun.

Date walk completed: